MW00365359

Praise for Mike Sager

"Wounded Warriors is entertaining and fascinating. It draws the reader into these lives; at the end of the book, you will find yourself changed in some way... You will remember these men that you read about long after putting this book to rest."

-- *Military Writers Society of America*

"Sager plays Virgil in the modern American Inferno... Compelling and stylish magazine journalism, rich in novelistic detail."

-- *Kirkus Reviews*

"Sager has written a gripping account of how these Marines are coping with their combat-altered lives. An experienced interviewer, he lets the Marines' stories speak for themselves...Powerful stuff."

--*Leatherneck, The Magazine of the Marines*

"Like his journalistic precursors Tom Wolfe and Hunter S. Thompson, Sager writes frenetic, off-kilter pop-sociological profiles of Americans in all their vulgarity and vitality...He writes with flair, but only in the service of an omnivorous curiosity and defies expectations in pieces that lesser writers would play for satire or sensationalism... A Whitmanesque ode to teeming humanity's mystical unity."

-- *New York Times Book Review*

"Sager's writing is strikingly perceptive. He writes like a novelist, stocking his stories with the details and observations other journalists might toss away."

-- KPBS Radio's "Culture Lust" blog

"Mike Sager is the best magazine journalist at work these days."

-- Austin American-Statesman

"A masterfully curated collection of that most exquisite of all curios, the human personality."

-- Cincinnati City Beat

"Sager writes in convincingly novelistic detail and supple, pinpoint prose about the inner lives of Americans."

-- Entertainment Weekly

"The pieces will move and entertain you."

— Esquire

"Wounded Warriors" was awarded:
» The American Author's Association Golden Quill Award
» The Military Writers Society of America Founder's Award

Other Books by Mike Sager

vetville

true stories of the u.s. marines at war and at home

THE SAGER GROUP

Artifex Te Adiuva

Vetville: True Stories of the U.S. Marines at War and at Home

Copyright © 2019 Mike Sager.

All rights reserved.
No part of this publication may be reproduced,
stored in a retrieval system,
or transmitted, in any form or by any means,
electronic, mechanical, photocopying,
recording, or otherwise, without the prior
written permission of the publisher.

Published in the United States of America.
Cover Designed by Stravinski Pierre and Siori
Kitajima, SF AppWorks LLC
Interior Designed by Siori Kitajima, SF
AppWorks LLC

Cataloging-in-Publication data for this book is
available from the Library of Congress.

ISBN-13: 978-1-950154-07-4
ISBN-10: 1-950154-07-6

Published by The Sager Group LLC
www.TheSagerGroup.net

vetville

true stories
of the
u.s. marines
at war and
at home

mike sager

THE SAGER GROUP

Artifex Te Adiuva

Semper Fi

Maj. William H. Sager, USMCR (Retired)
July 13, 1919-January 12, 2019

Sgt. Marvin M. Sager, USMCR
August 15, 1929-March 30, 2011

Table of Contents

Author's Note

In one of my earliest memories, I'm sitting on the top step of my grandmother's attic. To one side of me is a box of my father's things. It is dusty up there and a little bit hot.

I'm studying with fascination an object I know now was a collar device worn by U.S. Marines—an eagle, globe and anchor. I'm wearing my dad's vintage garrison cap, arranged on my head at a jaunty tilt. Nearby are a pair of sergeant's insignias. Even at my age, even without explanation, I sense the significance of these objects.

My dad was not one to tell personal stories. He was more of a listener who kept his own counsel. I do know he joined the Marine Corps Reserve during the Korean War. He was a junior in college at the time, a biology major, pre-med. He went through basic training at the Marine Corps Recruit Depot, Parris Island. In his graduation photo, he doesn't appear to be especially happy—he looks kind of absent, frankly; you might call it a half-mile stare. From there, he was assigned to a detachment of researchers aboard Camp Lejeune, North Carolina. Of his time there, I've only ever heard this: He worked on a team developing a new kind of body armor. Part of his duty to the nation involved fitting the prototype vests on sheep procured for the purpose... and then shooting the sheep with various firearms to see how well the design performed.

I would later learn to identify the lasting influence of his service in the corps. His proud and erect posture, shoulders back. His polite but formal way with strangers. The way he lined up his clothes so precisely in his bureau drawers and in his closet, as if he was awaiting a surprise inspection. His dress shirt was always perfectly pleated and secured inside his trousers; at meals, he'd unbutton a few buttons and stow away his tie to avoid stains. He often carried his wallet in his sock. He shaved every day, even weekends. Until the time of his death, at eighty-one, he called the bathroom the *head*.

It would be some time before my Uncle Buddy figured

significantly in my life. Maj. William H. Sager, USMCR (Retired), was my Dad's youngest uncle, ten years older than he.

While my dad served honorably, as I believe he did most everything in his life, Uncle Buddy was a genuine devil dog. He joined the Marines in 1939, attended officer training at Quantico, VA, and fought in pitched battles with the 1st Marine Division in Guadalcanal. After returning home to recover from a bad case of malaria, Uncle Buddy volunteered for duty in the mid-1940s with the Sino-American Cooperative Operation (SACO), a secret organization made up of volunteers from various U.S. armed services who performed covert activities in China—which included training Chinese guerillas and collecting intelligence. He later went to law school and had a distinguished career working as an attorney for the Federal Government.

Though I saw him at family gatherings and shared a table on occasion with his three kids, I didn't have much contact with Uncle Buddy until after college, when I moved to Washington, DC, to attend law school. My grandfather, Harry H. Sager, was an attorney. He died while I was in college. In my twenty-one-year-old mind, his legacy was among the main reasons I'd chosen to study the law.

Uncle Buddy was my grandfather's youngest brother. Two weeks into law school classes, I visited him at his downtown DC office. I already knew I didn't want to be a lawyer. I already had a dream: I wanted to become a writer. I was only attending law school so I would have, in my parents' words, "something to fall back on" when writing didn't pan out—a career I couldn't get going on until *after* I finished the three years of mind-numbing grad school. It seemed like a huge waste of time. I didn't know what to do.

Or I did know what to do. But first, in lieu of my grandfather's blessing, I think I needed Uncle Buddy's okay to carry on.

I will be forever grateful that he encouraged me to go for it.

***

Throughout my career, the majority of my stories have been assigned by editors. Because of this, I've covered a wide variety of topics. I have no particular beat; I'm a generalist. What distinguishes my work has always been more about the approach and the presentation.

So it has been quite by coincidence over the years that I found myself writing often about servicemen and women and their lives and issues.

As a newspaper reporter, I did dozens of stories about military subjects: Veterans' and Memorial Day spot news and features, funerals at Arlington National Cemetery, interviews with admirals and generals and enlisted men and women, visits to the Pentagon and most major military facilities in the DC area. I did a series about the Navy in Norfolk and another about my three weeks sailing aboard the U.S. Coast Guard's tall ship, the USCGC Eagle, a 295-foot barque used for training.

Later, as a magazine writer on a Marine Corps-sponsored junket, I spent a few days at Parris Island, where I met recruits and watched training. I took my turn at shooting range, the obstacle course, the rappelling wall, the mess hall. Through it all, I felt strongly my father's presence, especially on my tour of the barracks. The head was a long line of commodes, open, no stalls. He was all of nineteen when he passed through. As I write this, my son is twenty-four.

Within the subset of my military reportage, I've spent the deepest amount of time with the men (and a few women) of the U.S. Marine Corps. Though I've never personally served my country's military effort, I guess you could say I'm a Marine by blood, a loyal family member. I do remember singing proudly the Marine Corps anthem on car trips with my Dad. Maybe this is part of the reason I felt, from the beginning, a natural affinity with the members of this exclusive branch of service. It is as if I was called to the task. *Vetville* collects the best of my stories about the Marine Corps. Together this tetralogy of long form pieces charts a life story arc of the modern Devil Dog.

It begins at Camp Pendleton, CA, on field exercises with Lieutenant Colonel Bob Sinclair and his BN One-Four—the 1st Battalion, 4th Marine Regiment—as they prepare to invade Afghanistan, the first wave of American combatants sent to war after the deadly terrorist attacks of 9/11. "You realize that your country has been attacked," he says. "You wanna strike back."

From there, we head to the Wounded Warriors Barracks at Camp Lejeune where we meet Ringo, Cybula, Wildman, Lieutenant Colonel Maxwell, and the rest of the men recuperating together at a unique barracks where wounded Marines harness their esprit de corps to help one another through emotional and physical recovery. We hear their battlefield stories of war and heroism. And their stories of injury and despair. And we discover the soft center that lives beneath the tough exterior shell of the Marine Corps mystique—a deep love of comrades and country. "Wounded Warriors" was awarded a number of awards, including The Military Writers Society of America Founder's Award.

In "Vetville," we visit a small farm in the mountains of Tennessee, where a Marine sergeant, in an effort to save himself and his brothers, has opened his doors to veterans whose deep wounds don't necessarily show. And, we catch up with John Cybula, one of the men encountered aboard the Wounded Warriors barracks. Without a supportive network around him, he has turned to drugs.

Finally, in "Fifty Grand in San Diego," we focus on the return to civilian life after the Corps, with a look at a modern version of the American Dream—an ex-Marine playing Mr. Mom and finding his silver cloud in a dirty diaper.

***

I guess it doesn't take much investigative reporting to figure out some of the reasons why I—the son of a man who loved and supported me mightily but spoke little of himself or his inner feelings—have spent pretty much the majority of my adult life interviewing and studying men unrelated to me.

Never for a moment do I forget, however, that what my father failed to pass along in the form of anecdotes, he passed along in character traits—among them a keen ability to listen and to empathize.

Uncle Buddy died recently at ninety-nine. We have stayed in touch through the years, mostly when I was seeking to access his steel trap of a brain. One of those people who possess a savant's facility to remember dates and events, he spent some of his retirement compiling and assembling histories of the Sager family and his military service. In the days before self-publishing, he proudly sent me each new spiral-bound copy-shop volume he accomplished, all of which helped me piece together a better understanding of my own history. I keep these special editions together in my library, laid flat to avoid warping. Sometimes I think: *Maybe he would have liked to have become a writer, too.* Of course, he was from a generation that was neither as spoiled nor as fortunate as mine. I strike these keys in his honor.

Like my dad and my great uncle, every Marine mentioned in this collection has played an important role in shaping the man I have become. I am still in touch with a number of the folks mentioned in these stories, and I am heartened to let you know that all of those I correspond with are thriving. Of course, there are others from whom I haven't heard. I pray they are well.

While I will never for a moment have the temerity to say I can understand exactly what it means to be a Marine or to face live combat, or that I can render with exact realism the delicate way life and feelings are constructed in the minds of other people, I have attempted in these stories to bring to light a true and accurate picture of the men and women depicted.

To all the Marines now and before, and especially those in this book, thank you for your service. And thank you for letting me in.

Semper Fi,

Mike Sager
La Jolla, CA

The Marine

Three months after 9/11, Lieutenant Colonel Bob Sinclair and his Marine battalion are in the first wave of American combatants headed to Afghanistan. "You realize that your country has been attacked," he says. "You wanna strike back."

D ragon Six is Oscar Mike, on the move to link up with Bandit. Foot-mobile along Axis Kim, he is leading a detachment of ten U.S. Marines across a stretch of desert scrub in the notional, oil-rich nation of Blueland. He walks at a steady rate of three klicks per hour, three kilometers, muscle memory after twenty-three years of similar forced humps though the toolies, his small, powerful body canted slightly forward, his ankles and knees a little sore, his dusty black Danner combat boots, size eight, crunching over branches and rocks and coarse sand.

His pale-blue eyes are bloodshot from lack of sleep. His face is camouflaged with stripes and splotches of greasepaint—green, brown, and black to match his woodland-style utilities, fifty-six dollars a set, worn in the field without skivvies underneath, a personal wardrobe preference known as going commando. Atop his Kevlar helmet rides a pair of goggles sheathed in an old sock. Around his neck hangs a heavy pair of rubberized binoculars. From his left hip dangles an olive-drab pouch. With every step, the pouch swings and hits his thigh, adding another faint, percussive thunk to the quiet symphony of his gear, the total weight of which is not taught and seldom discussed. Inside the pouch is a gas mask for NBC attacks—nuclear, biological, or chemical weapons. Following an attack, when field gauges show the air to be safe once again for breathing, regulations call for the senior Marine to choose one man to remove his mask and hood. After ten minutes, if the man shows no ill effects, the rest of the Marines can begin removing theirs.

The temperature is 82 degrees. The air is thick and humid. Sounds of distant fire travel on the wan breeze: the boom and rumble of artillery, the pop and crackle of small arms. He is leading his men in a northwesterly direction, headed for an unimproved road designated Phase Line Rich. There, he will rendezvous with Bravo Company, radio call sign Bandit, one of five companies under his command, nearly 900 men, armed with weapons ranging from M16A2 rifles to Humvee-mounted TOW missile launchers. In his gloved right hand, he carries a map case fashioned from cardboard and duct tape—the cardboard scavenged from a box of MREs, meals ready-to-eat, high-tech field rations that cook themselves when water is added. Clipped to the map case is a rainbow assortment of felt-tip pens, the colors oddly garish against the setting. His 9mm Beretta sidearm is worn just beneath his right chest, high on his abdomen. The holster is secured onto his H harness, a pair of mesh suspenders anchored to the war belt around his waist— which itself holds magazine pouches with spare ammo and twin canteens. Altogether, this load-bearing apparatus is known as deuce gear, as in U.S. Government Form No. 782, the receipt a Marine was once required to sign upon issuance. These days, the Corps is computerized.

Near his left clavicle, also secured to his H-harness—which is worn atop his flak vest—is another small pouch. Inside, he keeps his Leatherman utility tool, his government-issue New Testament, a bag of Skittles left over from an MRE, and a tin of Copenhagen snuff, a medium-sized dip of which is evident at this moment in the bulge of his bottom lip, oddly pink in contrast to his thick camo makeup, and in the bottom lips of most of the men in his detachment, a forward-command element known as the Jump. They march slue-footed in a double-file formation through California sage and coyote bush and fennel, the smell pungent and spicy, like something roasting in a gourmet oven, each man silent and serious, deliberate in movement, eyes tracking left and right, as trained, each man taking a moment now and then, without breaking stride, to purse his lips and spit a stream of brownish liquid onto the ground, the varied styles of their expectorations somehow befitting, a metaphor for each personality, a metaphor, seemingly, for the Marine Corps itself: a tribe of like minds in different bodies, a range of shapes and sizes and colors, all wearing the same haircut and uniform, all hewing to the same standards and customs, yet still a collection of individuals, each with his own particular style of spitting tobacco juice, each with his own particular life to give for his country.

In the center of his flak vest—hot and heavy, designed to stop shrapnel but not bullets or knives—is a metal pin about the size of a dime, his insignia of rank, a silver oak leaf. Ever since he was young growing up on the outskirts of Seattle, the second of four sons born to a department store manager and a missionary's daughter, Robert O. Sinclair always wanted to be a Marine. Now, at age forty, he has reached the rank of lieutenant colonel. He has what many consider to be the ultimate job for an infantry officer in the Corps, the command of his own battalion, in this case BN One-Four—the 1st Battalion, 4th Marine Regiment. A proud unit with a distinguished history, the One-Four saw its first action in 1916, during the Banana Wars in the Dominican Republic. In the late twenties, the 4th Marines became known as the China Regiment when it was sent to Shanghai to protect American interests. During World War II, the One-Four was part of a larger force that surrendered to the Japanese at Corregidor. Its colors were burned; the survivors became POWs, forced to endure the infamous Bataan Death March. Re-formed two years later, the unit avenged itself in the first wave of landings on Guam. It has since fought in Vietnam, Desert Storm, and Somalia.

Come January, Sinclair and the One-Four—expanded to include tanks, artillery, amphibious and light-armored vehicles, engineers, and 350 additional troops—will ship out on three Navy amphibious assault vessels as the 13th MEU (SOC), Marine Expeditionary Unit (Special Operations Capable), bound for the western Pacific and the Persian Gulf, ready for immediate action, fully equipped to wage combat for fifteen days without resupply or reinforcement, a unit precisely suited to a war against terrorism. "We specialize in conducting raids," says Sinclair. "We're tailor-made for special ops. We're trained to get in, hit a target, kill the enemy, and friggin' pull back to our ships again. We can go by helo. We can infiltrate by land. We can go ashore conventionally. We can put together anything. We're ready to do whatever it takes."

At the moment, in Marine lingo, it is twenty-four sixteen thirty uniform May zero one, 4:30 in the afternoon on May 24, 2001, well before the prospect of going to war suddenly became real and imminent this fall. It is the fourth day of something called the Battalion FEX—a field exercise, on-the-job training for Sinclair and his Marines. Truth be told, this is the first chance Sinclair has ever had to take his entire battalion out for a spin. Eight months ago, he had a lower rank and a different job in another unit somewhere else. Eight months ago, 90 percent of the men in his battalion were somewhere else; a good percentage of them had only recently graduated from high school. All told, between the time he took the flag of the One-Four—a dragon wrapped around a dagger on a blue diamond; the motto: Whatever It Takes—and the day this January or sooner when he and his men and all their equipment steam out of San Diego Harbor—wives and families and a brass band left behind on the dock—Sinclair will have had only eighteen months to build from scratch a crack fighting force, trained for every contingency from humanitarian aid to police action to strategic guerrilla raids to full-scale invasion. He has seven more months to get the bugs out. There is much to be done.

And so it is that Bob Sinclair is Oscar Mike across a stretch of desert scrub in the notional country of Blueland, which is actually in the state of California at Camp Pendleton, the largest amphibious training base in the world, spread across 125,000 rugged and breathtaking acres along the Pacific coastline. In ten mikes or so, ten minutes, over the next rise, Sinclair will link up with Bandit, the main effort in this five-phase operational. From there, Sinclair will lead his Marines into the mountains, toward a BP, a battle position, high atop a steep, no-name hill. At zero four hundred hours, with the pop and arc of a white double-star-burst flare, the battle will commence: a non-supported, nonilluminated night attack against the invading enemy forces of Orangeland, dug in at a critical crossroads, eyes on the Jesara oil fields.

Or that is the play, anyway. Like the bubbas say: A plan is only good until the first shot is fired. Sometimes not even until then.

***

At Phase Line Rich, Sinclair and his men take cover in a stand of high weeds. The four young grunts who form his security element—a corporal and three privates, pimples showing through camo paint—employ along a tight circular perimeter. They assume prone positions on the deck in the rocky sand, cheeks resting against the stocks of their weapons, three M16A2 rifles and an M249 SAW, Squad Automatic Weapon, a 5.56mm light machine gun with a removable bipod.

The ground is riddled with gopher mounds, busy with ants, bugs, and small lizards. Three types of rattlesnakes inhabit the area, along with scorpions, coyotes, roadrunners, and mountain lions. Overhead, against a backdrop of rugged mountains and gray sky, a red-tailed hawk backpedals its wings, suspended in flight, talons flexed, fixing a target far below.

Sinclair sits with his legs crossed Indian-style. A fly buzzes around his head; bees alight upon the intricate yellow flowers of the black mustard weeds. Filled to capacity, his assault pack and his ass pack form a backrest, a comfortable pillow on which to lounge. Inside the packs, among other items, he keeps a roll of toilet paper; extra socks; reserve tins of Copenhagen; map templates; his NVGs, night-vision goggles; his CamelBak, a one-gallon water reservoir with a long drinking tube attached; and his MOPP suit and booties, Mission Oriented Protective Posture, Marine lingo for the overclothes worn with the gas mask in case of NBC attack.

Five feet six inches tall, Sinclair has a quick, high-pitched giggle and bulging biceps, a Marine Corps tattoo on each shoulder. He is, in the words of one of his officers, "a good human being who's able to be a taskmaster." He has a pretty wife, his second, a baby son, and partial custody of his eleven-year-old stepson. They live among civilians on a cul-de-sac in a cookie-cutter subdivision about thirty minutes from the base, a black Isuzu Trooper and a black Volvo station wagon parked side by side in the driveway. He loves fishing, attends church regularly, prays before eating his MREs in the field.

Though Sinclair was once lampooned in a skit as the Angry Little Man, he is known to his Marines as a teacher and a father figure. Above all, he is known as a bubba, a fellow grunt. Unlike most Marine officers, Sinclair joined the Corps right out of high school. He spent the summer in boot camp in San Diego, then went off to Western Washington University. Following graduation (he majored in political science), upon completion of his basic officer training, Sinclair was asked to list three career choices. He wrote *infantry* three times. He was chewed out by his CO for disobeying orders—if the Marine Corps says three choices, it damn well means three—but it was worth it to him to make the point.

At twenty-two, as a lieutenant, Sinclair became a rifle platoon commander. At twenty-nine, as a captain, he was a company commander in an infantry battalion similar to the One-Four and saw action in Somalia and Rwanda. In his early thirties, as a major, he served time as both a key member of a general's staff and as the director of the Infantry Officer Course in Quantico, Virginia. Today, as CO of the One-Four, he is known for his attention to detail, his almost monkish expertise in battlefield tactics and techniques. Important also is his reputation for pushing down power to the NCOs, for delegating authority to the noncommissioned officers, the sergeants and the corporals, an essential managerial concept in this bottom-heavy organization. The smallest of all the services—about 170,000 compared with the Army's 480,000 (800,000 including reserves)—the Marines also have the lowest officer-to-enlisted ratio, one-to-nine, compared with the Army's one-to-five. More than half of the Corps is composed of the three lowest pay grades—lance corporals, privates first class, and privates. Every year, more than 30 percent of the enlisted ranks muster out and return to civilian life. Discounting career officers and NCOs, that means a complete recycling of bodies about every three years.

Now, as Sinclair sits in the weeds near Phase Line Rich, dark clouds gather ominously over the mountains. "Guess we're in for a nice little hike," he says, flashing his trademark smile, toothy and overlarge.

"Yes, sir!" sings out Sergeant Major, sitting to his right. John Hamby, forty, is the ranking noncommissioned officer in the One-Four, the most senior of all the enlisted, though still junior to the greenest second lieutenant. A good ol' boy from Georgia with a booming gravel voice, he is always at Sinclair's side, offering advice and support, implementing orders, watchdogging the interests of his men. Asked about his favorite Marine memories, he thinks a moment, names three: the day, at age twenty-nine, that he received his high school diploma, the 4.0 valedictorian of his class; the day his father pinned his sergeant major chevrons to his collar; the day, when he was stationed in Vienna as an embassy guard, that his son was born by emergency C-section.

"Those peaks behind Basilone Road are gonna be a ball buster," Sinclair says. "Holy Moses!"

"Been there many times," Sergeant Major says. He spits a stream of brownish liquid into the weeds. "Character builder, sir."

"It won't be as steep as yesterday, but it's a lot friggin' higher," Sinclair says, his flat Northwestern accent flavored with a bit of Southern drawl, affected to a greater or lesser extent by most Marine officers, no matter what their regional origins—homage, perhaps, to the antebellum notion of the Southern gentleman, upon whom the patriotic ideal of a young American military leader was modeled. He spits a stream of juice, then kicks some dirt over the wet spot on the ground, covering it up.

"You would think there'd be a limit as to how much character you can build, sir. But I ain't reached it yet."

"Oo-rah, Sergeant Major."

"Ain't that right, Colón?" Sergeant Major cuffs the shoulder of the nervous young radio operator sitting behind Sinclair, nearly knocking him over. Private First Class Mike Colón is twenty years old, a slight youth just this side of pretty: five feet four with long curly lashes. The twelve-pound radio he's carrying—a one nineteen foxtrot SINCGARS, a single-channel ground-and-airborne radio system—fits with some difficulty into his assault pack. The ten-foot whip-style antenna makes balance difficult. Thirty minutes into the hump, he has already slapped Sinclair on the helmet several times with the thick rod of rubber-coated steel.

Born in Puerto Rico, raised in the ghetto of Holyoke, Massachusetts, Colón speaks English with the singsong rhythms of his home island. Both of his earlobes are pierced, a remnant of his days with the Latin Kings. Six months ago, Colón was breaking rocks with a ten-pound sledge in the CCU, the Correctional Custody Unit at Camp Pendleton, busted down to private for drinking in the barracks. It was his third offense; the Old Man could have run him out of the Corps. But Sinclair prides himself on being able to judge his Marines, to see into their souls. As he likes to say: "You can't friggin' command from behind a damn desk." In battle, you have to know what to expect from your men. That's the whole reason they practice everything so many times. That's the whole reason he's out here on the Jump rather than back in the rear, commanding from a camp chair in the relative comfort of the COC, the Combat Operations Center, a big black tent with a generator, lights, computers, and a banquet-sized coffee urn.

Sinclair saw something in Colón, and Colón responded: He was down but he never dropped his pack, as the bubbas say. Now he has found himself assigned as the Old Man's radio operator. He darts a look at Sergeant Major. Privilege in the Marine Corps is often a two-edged sword. Had he not been so honored by this assignment, he'd be back at the COC himself, pulling radio watch. He aims a stream of brownish juice toward the ground. A little bit dribbles down his chin, onto his flak vest. "A definite character builder, Sergeant Major."

Sinclair twists around, flashes Colón his smile. "There ya go, stud," he sings encouragingly.

"Here comes Bandit right now," announces the OpsO, the operations officer, indicating the lead element of Bravo Company, coming around a bend double file.

Major Minter Bailey Ralston IV—Uncle Minty to his friends—is Dragon Three to Sinclair's Dragon Six. He plans and coordinates all battalion movements in the field. Thirty-two years old, a strapping six feet two, he's a graduate of the Virginia Military Institute. Since 1856, every Minter Bailey Ralston before him had been a pharmacist. Growing up in the tiny town of Westin, West Virginia, the only boy of four children, he set his sights early on the Marines. "John Wayne and comic books took me to the dark side at a very early age," he says.

Blond and blue-eyed, with circles under his eyes, Ralston was up all last night on the laptop computer in the COC, pecking out Battalion Frag Order zero one tach four, the detailed, six-page battle plan for tonight's movement. Grimacing, he pops two large pills without water. Three weeks ago, he underwent surgery on his right calf muscle. He is not yet cleared for exercise of any kind.

Sitting next to Major Ralston is the FSC, the fire-support coordinator, Major Randy Page. Six feet four with green eyes, thirty-four years old, Page hails from Wagon Wheel, New Mexico, population fifty. His job is coordinating artillery and other weapons fire to support the grunts on the ground. Married with no kids, a foreign-film buff, a self-professed computer geek, Page loves being in the field. His favorite Marine moment is a snapshot: "You're in the rain, you're on a knee, and everyone's just miserable. And you just kinda look around and it feels like—you feel like crap because you're cold or hot or wet or whatever—but it just feels good."

Now Page hoists himself off the deck. He scans the horizon, taking a deep draft of the spicy air. "Looks like that fog is comin' in a little early, sir."

"Roger that, Major Page," Sinclair says, grunting a bit as he rises, as men of a certain age begin to do.

"On your feet, Marines," growls Sergeant Major. He kicks playfully at the boot of Lance Corporal Joseph Gray, the other radio operator on the Jump. Gray has been dragging lately. He's newly married to a very young Cuban girl. There are troubles at home, a baby on the way. Sergeant Major reaches down and offers Gray a helping hand. "Move it, Devil Dog," he barks.

***

After a long, steep climb—the last bit a 70-degree slope through sharp thistles—Dragon Jump and Bandit are in place on the summit of No Name Hill, looking down upon Battalion Objectives Four and Five. Huddled together in the pitch-dark, Sinclair and his men are totally assed out. They sit in rocky sand, on a firebreak cut across the topographical crest of the hill. A cloud bank has settled over them. Visibility is nil; their NVGs, which use ambient light, are inoperable. It is cold and wet and quiet, the silence broken only by the beep and crackle of the SINCGARS radios.

The time is zero one thirty hours. According to intelligence, there is a company-minus, about 150 men, of Orangeland forces dug in around the two key crossroads in the valley below, just to the northeast of No Name Hill, 1,500 meters away as the crow flies. Scout/sniper reports have the enemy armed with AK-47 rifles, light and medium machine guns, and 82mm mortars. Based upon documents taken from the body of a notionally dead officer (members of the One-Four's H&S company, headquarters and service, are playing the role of the enemy), there is reason to believe that the Orangeland forces, members of the dictator's elite Revolutionary Guard, will attempt to hold their positions at all costs.

Though the original frag order tasked Bravo Company as the main effort of the attack, it has become clear that the plan is no longer viable. Not apparent on the contour map was the fact that the northeast face of No Name Hill is a sheer cliff. There is no way Sinclair is going to order a company of green Marines down the side without rappelling systems. Likewise, the firebreak is useless as an avenue of approach; cut by giant bulldozers, one hundred feet wide, that piece of terrain is completely exposed—the face sloping down gradually onto the objective like a ski run.

Because they're here to learn how to think on the fly, Sinclair has ordered Ralston to recast the attack, a laborious process that began with Ralston—owing to the blackout conditions in effect—lying for a time beneath his rain poncho, his red-lensed flashlight in one hand, a pen in the other, writing up formal orders for the new attack, composing sentences such as: O/O ATK TO DESTROY EN VIC BN OBJ 4. Once completed, the orders were disseminated via radio down the chain of command. Upon receiving his orders, each Marine made a few notes for himself in his olive-drab journal, part of his required gear.

The new play goes like this: Charlie Company, down in the valley, formerly the supporting effort, becomes the main effort in the attack. It will move across the desert floor, around the bottom of No Name Hill, then turn left in a bent-L formation. Upon seeing the signal flare—a green double star burst—it will attack the enemy's flank. Bravo Company will remind on No Name Hill in a support-by-fire position. In addition, Sinclair has called up the CAAT platoon, the Combined Anti-Armor Team, a motorized unit comprising Humvee-mounted .50-caliber machine guns and wire-guided TOW missile launchers.

While Charlie Company moves into its new position—difficult in the dark without NVGs, foot mobile at the excruciatingly slow rate of 500 meters an hour through the difficult terrain—Sinclair and his men hunker down on the firebreak atop No Name Hill, a dark circle of faceless shadows enveloped in a fine, cold mist.

Lounging against his assault pack, Sinclair's cammies beneath his flak vest are sopping with sweat. He's cold and tired, and his knees ache. He's "dawggone friggin' miserable"; he's happy as he can be. This is what he signed up for. He's glad he chose to go out on the Jump tonight, down and dirty with the men, the more miserable the better, commanding with his eyes instead of a radio handset. There's a purity to being in the field. It helps you keep your edge. It helps you keep your sense of perspective. You learn not to take your lifestyle and your freedoms for granted. You learn not to care so much about what year the wine was bottled, what brand of clothing you wear, all that horseshit that people think is oh-so-civilized. Being out here, you learn to appreciate the simple things, like just how great it is to sit on a toilet to take a dump.

Over the years, Sinclair has endured conditions much worse than these. He's been in the desert in Kuwait, 130 degrees. He's looked into the eyes of starving infants in Somalia. He's rescued civilians from the American embassy in Rwanda. And he's seen men die; he's written impotent letters home to inconsolable mothers after a firefight with Somali thugs in pickup trucks. It's bad out here tonight on No Name Hill, but it's not so bad. In real-world time, he's a thirty-minute drive from home. Come tomorrow evening, he'll be in his living room with Jessie for their fifth wedding anniversary— the first such celebration he's ever been able to attend.

"I read the other day that gas prices have gone up 149 percent in the last year," Sinclair says, trying to pass the time.

"The cost of living here has gotten to be more expensive than Hawaii," says Page, seated to Sinclair's left. His words come out a little slurry. He chides himself for not sleeping last night. He shakes his head, trying to rid the cobwebs.

"Guess there's no chance we're gettin' a raise anytime soon," Ralston says. Though no one can see it, he has his boot off, an instant ice pack on his badly swollen calf. He missed the last big exercise because of his surgery—if you can't do your job, the Marines will replace you. Someday Ralston would like to be in Sinclair's boots; this is too good a billet to let go because of a little pain. Or that's what he thought. Now the calf is throbbing. *Could I be happy as a civilian?* he asks himself, only half kidding.

"The president has already submitted his supplemental budget this year, so we're looking at zero three at the earliest for any kind of COLA," Sinclair says, meaning cost-of-living adjustment, his monkish side still apparent through his own physical exhaustion. Oddly missing from his encyclopedia of knowledge is the exact amount of his salary. For that information, you must see Jessie. He draws $72,000 a year, plus an additional $1,700 a month for food and housing.

"That's just peachy," Sergeant Major says. He pulls down about $45,000 a year, plus $1,500 a month for food and housing. "Maybe I'll trade in my car and get a beat-up old Volkswagen. Put the wife on the street corner."

"We won't quote you on that, Sergeant Major," Sinclair says.

"Definitely not," says Page.

"Even I don't go *that* far," Sergeant Major says. His voice softens, grows sentimental, like a guy talking to the bartender late at night. "There ain't none like her. She's mine. We have our times, but it wouldn't be no fun if there wasn't a little challenge."

"Damn," says Ralston. "The wind's kickin' up."

"I'm kinda hoping that stink is you and not me," Sergeant Major drawls. "You know it's time to take a shower when you can smell your own ass."

"Jeez, *Louise*, Sergeant Major!" Sinclair says. "Thanks for sharin'."

***

At zero three fifty atop No Name Hill, the rain has subsided; the clouds remain.

Sinclair and his men are on their feet now, helmeted shadows milling between two Humvees. Parked on the firebreak, on the crest of the hill, each of the four-wheel-drive vehicles is fitted with a TOW missile launcher and an infrared sight. In a few minutes, when the liquid nitrogen in the mechanism reaches a temperature of -318 degrees, Sinclair will be able to look through a rubber-capped eyepiece and see the heat signatures of his otherwise-invisible foes, tiny red human forms in the valley far below. Mounted to turrets atop the roots of the vehicles, the TOW sights emit a loudish ticking noise, a strangely familiar sound, like the timer on a heat lamp in a hotel bathroom.

"Spare a dip, Sergeant Major?"

"Sorry, Major Page, I'm plum out."

"What about you, OpsO?"

"I was just gonna ask you."

"Well, isn't this a fine damn thing," Sergeant Major says. He pauses a beat, thinking. A few days ago, back at Camp Horno—the One-Four's compound at Pendleton—Sergeant Major needed a sleeping bag for a reporter to take on the FEX. Informed by supply that the battalion was fresh out of sleeping bags, Sergeant Major ordered the lance corporal on the other end of the line to *shit* a sleeping bag *posthaste*. The bag was delivered in ten minutes.

Now, five days into the FEX, twelve hours into this movement, what Sergeant Major needs—what they all need—is a good whack of nicotine. He turns to Sinclair. "What about you, sir?"

Sinclair pulls off his right glove with his teeth, reaches into the pouch secured over the left side of his chest. He takes out his tin of Copenhagen, opens it. "A few dregs," he says, disappointed. Then he brightens. "Criminy! Check my assault pack!"

Sinclair turns his back and Sergeant Major unzips him, rummages carefully through his gear. Though entirely offhand, it is an intimate act. He comes out with a fresh tin. "You aint' been holdin' out on us now, sir, have you?"

"Pass it around, by all means!"

"An officer and a gentleman," Sergeant Major declares.

"Anything for my Marines," Sinclair says. He looks around the loose circle of his men, the faceless shadowy figures so distinctly recognizable, even in the murky gloom. In boot camp, there are no walls between the shitters in the latrine—that's how close you get to the other guys. And when you have to lead them, when your word is literally their command, well... it's hard to find a way to express it. Eight months into his tenure as the CO of the One-Four, Sinclair finds himself stepping back every now and then and thinking, *Dawggone, I still can't believe I have this authority!* You go through the years, gaining experience, working hard, moving up. And then one day *you're* the Old Man. But you still feel like you; you're the same as always—a little bit afraid of fucking up. It makes you want to be careful. Not cautious, just more careful to consider things from every imaginable side. Bottom line is a most awesome fact: He has lives in his hands.

When he looks at one of *his* Marines, Sinclair doesn't care what age or color he is, what MOS or billet he occupies. He doesn't care if he's a wrench turner down in the motor pool or one of his company commanders. If he didn't need that man in the One-Four, the Marine Corps wouldn't have assigned him. Every truck driver hauling water and chow to the grunts in the field; the comm guys running wire and maintaining the nets; the eighteen-year-old rifleman toting a 60mm mortar launcher over his shoulders, sucking on his water tube like a pacifier as he humps up a hill—

they're all important to him as a commander. They all need to know that Sinclair's thinking, *Hey, stud, I know that job may not seem fun or exciting, but I need your skills to make this whole thing work.*

"So what do we do now?" asks Sergeant Major. He takes a pinch and passes it on. He's feeling better already.

"We could fight this little battle," says Ralton.

"I make it zero three fifty nine," says Page, taking the tin from Ralston.

"I know," Sinclair says. He rubs his hands together greedily. "Who can we meritoriously promote?"

"Excellent idea, sir!" Sergeant Major says.

"How about Rivers?" suggests Page.

"He's ready?" asks Sinclair.

"Definitely, sir."

"What do you think, Colón?"

"Definitely, sir," says the radio operator, taking a dip, passing the tin.

"All right, good to go," Sinclair says, inserting his own pinch of dip between lip and gum. He steps up onto the fat tire of the Humvee, swings himself into the turret. "We'll just take care of business here," he calls down from his perch, "and then—"

Now there comes the distinct explosive pop of a flare, and everyone turns to see. A green double star burst, lovely and bright and sparkling, it floats down toward earth on its invisible parachute, as languid as an autumn leaf falling from a tree, illuminating the target below in surreal shades of magnesium green.

Down in the valley, Charlie Company opens fire. There is the crackle of small arms shooting blank rounds, clusters of bright muzzle flashes against the dark, the loud cacophony of voices that accompanies a firefight—men on both sides shouting orders and epithets as the battle is waged at close quarters.

Atop No Name Hill, fore and aft of the vehicles, platoons from Bravo Company are set along different elevations of the firebreak. As this is only an exercise, the budget for the FEX is limited. The men of Bravo Company have been told not to expend their blank rounds. They have humped ten difficult miles in the last twelve hours to get into position for this attack, through fields of cactus and thistles, up steep slopes and through ravines, weighted with myriad weapon systems and gear. They have shivered in their own sweat in the fine, cold rain, faces in the sand with the insects and the weeds, fighting boredom, dehydration, fatigue. They have done everything the Old Man has asked, and they have done it without question or excuse or complaint. On order, they open fire.

"Bang bang bang bang BANG!" they shout into the darkness, 200 strong, every shape and color, all wearing the same haircuts and uniforms, their voices echoing across the valley, a shitstorm of simulated plunging fire raining down death upon Orangeland's elite Revolutionary Guard: "Bang bang bang bang BANG!"

***

By zero seven thirty, the enemy has been vanquished.

Dragon Jump and Bandit have humped down the firebreak, consolidated with Charlie Company. Together, they occupy Battalion Objectives Four and Five.

It is cool and overcast. The two key crossroads are little more than dirt trails etched through the valley. Sinclair and his men mill about. No Name Hill looms above them, impossibly high from this vantage point, a scrubby, humpbacked ridge stippled with boulders, the firebreak running like a raw scar over the crest. Colón and Gray and the other enlisted are circled up, passing a rumpled menthol cigarette that Colón has found in his pack. Sinclair and Sergeant Major lean against a Humvee, shooting the shit with the battalion XO, the executive officer, Major Rich Weede. Thirty-seven years old, a graduate of VMI, Weede is Dragon Five to Sinclair's Dragon Six, responsible for many of the nuts-and-bolts issues of command. Since 1935, there has continuously been a Weede on active duty in the Marine Corps. His grandfather retired as a lieutenant general. His father retired as a colonel. His brother is a captain.

Sinclair has logged only about six hours of sleep over the last five days. His eyelids are sprung like window shades. His smile seems plastered onto his face. His knees feel disjointed, as if he's walking on eggshells. He feels thready and insubstantial, oddly gelatinous, a little queasy, as if he's treading water in a vitreous sea of adrenaline and dopamine, nicotine, and excess stomach acid. Now the drifting conversation has turned toward a mutual friend of Weede and Sinclair's, a retired officer.

"So he's got a beer distributorship?" Sinclair asks, his voice tight and forced.

"Every day he's gettin' invitations to fuckin' golf tournaments," Weede says, breaking out a couple of cheroot cigars.

"That's like the time I met this guy through my father-in-law," says Sergeant Major, accepting a cheroot, taking a bite. "He flies me down to Texas to play golf at his country club, and we played a round, and then he takes me over to his warehouse. He tells me how he's having problems with his employees, how he can't get them motivated. And then he says, 'Your father-in-law seems to think you're pretty good at that shit. You want a job? I'll make it well worth your while.'"

"I'da friggin' asked how well," Sinclair says, taking a bite of his cheroot, working it down to his gum.

"That's like Gunner Montoya," Weede says, blowing a smoke ring. "He said he told the guy, 'I'm a Marine gunner, I don't know a friggin' thing about this business.' And the guy tells him, 'You're a Marine, you can manage this shit, trust me.'"

"The salary kicks up to a hundred grand after a year," Sergeant Major says. "He put in his papers this month."

"I can't even fathom that kinda money," Sinclair says. He looks off toward No Name Hill, shaking his head.

OpsO Ralston limps over, and Weede offers him a cheroot. "Time to head back to the barn, sir," Ralston says to Sinclair. It's a three-hour hump back to Camp Horno.

"We goin' up Sheepshit Hill, sir?" asks Sergeant Major.

"Only the best for my Devil Dogs!" Sinclair sings.

"They'll be back by this afternoon and too tired to bitch," drawls Sergeant Major. "Then they'll get up tomorrow all sore and thinking, *Fuuuuuuuck!* But come Sunday, their tune'll change. It'll be: *That wasn't shit!*"

"Twenty-four hours from now they'll be bragging about how tough it was," Sinclair says. He spits a stream, kicks some dirt over the wet spot.

"You know," Sergeant Major says, "I didn't sign up for infantry. I was gonna be a mechanic."

"Well, I did. All I ever wanted to be was a grunt."

"Then I guess all your dreams have come true, sir."

"Oo-rah, Sergeant Major."

***

On a sunny afternoon a few weeks later, Sinclair is sitting beneath a striped umbrella on the patio behind his house. He is barefoot, dressed in a tank top and surfer shorts. His face and neck are deeply tanned; his shoulders and legs are milky white. Even on his day off, he sports a fresh shave. In his mind, he's never off duty; he's a Marine every hour of every day. He doesn't even go to Home Depot without shaving first. He has his whitewall-style haircut trimmed weekly, seven dollars a pop.

Sinclair was up early today, ripping out the roots of a tree in the front yard that had begun to encroach upon the sidewalk. For a tool he used an old bolo knife he bought in the Philippines when he was a second lieutenant. A short machete made from dense steel, the thing hasn't been sharpened in twenty years and it's still the best dawggone piece of cuttin' gear he's got. Now that the tree roots have been vanquished, Sinclair needs to repipe the irrigation in that area. Not to mention all the other chores. His tidy two-story house, decorated in earth tones, is filled with projects not yet completed: a partially painted wall, a set of dining-room chairs only half reupholstered. An epic list maker, he has yellow Post-its everywhere at home and at work. He's got a lot to do before January.

At home, Jessie is the idea guy; the Old Man is the grunt. When he comes through the front door, he always says, "Just tell me what to do. I don't want to make *any* decisions." Jessie and Bob met on a blind date eight years ago. He was a captain then, company commander; her sister was dating his radio operator. They went to a Japanese restaurant. When he returned home that night, Bob looked in the mirror and told himself he had found the woman he was going to marry. Two days after their date, Jessie came down with the flu. Bob drove an hour to bring her some medicine. "I could tell right then he was a keeper," she says.

Jessie sees Bob as being tough in his professional life, yet very tender in his personal life. He is honest and sincere, a mature man with a lot of integrity, very different from other men, a grownup in every way. When she was laid up in the hospital before their son, Seth, was born, he took off work and camped out in the room with her for an entire week. Five years into their marriage, he still refers to her as "my bride."

Soon after they began dating, Bob went off on a six-month deployment. Jessie sent him care packages filled with Gummy Bears and pistachio nuts. They wrote letters every day. She didn't know where he was, exactly. Somewhere out on a ship. Bob is an awesome letter writer. He would write about what he did that day and how he was feeling about stuff. And then there were the romantic parts. Those were her favorite.

One night when he was on the float, Jessie's phone rang. It was Bob. "I just wanted to tell you I love you," he said casually, and Jessie thought, *Uh-oh, I don't like the sound of this.* Before he hung up, he mentioned that she should watch CNN the next day. Sure enough, there were the Marines, evacuating civilians from the embassy in Rwanda.

Following his deployment, Bob was transferred to Quantico, Virginia, for three years. The couple maintained a long-distance relationship, getting married along the way, holding their reception at the Japanese restaurant where they'd had their first date. Though she doesn't want to say it in so many words, Jessie is not looking forward to this deployment. Bob's been home now for a long stretch. She's used to having him around. He's funny, he's good company, he has sexy arms and a nice smile. He doesn't mind doing the vacuuming. He thinks everything she cooks is delicious. And though he's not much into television—not even sports—he's happy to sit with her and watch her shows: *Friends, Ed, The West Wing, ER,*

Malcolm in the Middle. When he goes away, it's always hardest in the beginning. Then she bucks up and gets in the groove; she just kind of goes about her business. In time, she even starts to enjoy being on her own—pretty much, anyway. It's funny, but having Bob gone so much has taught her just how secure a person she really is. In that way, the Marine Corps has been good for her as well.

This time the float will be a little different for the Sinclairs. They'll have email. And because he's the battalion commander and she's the Key Volunteer Adviser—informally in charge of overseeing all the dependents—he'll be calling her by telephone weekly.

The biggest difference, of course, is Seth, eighteen months old, a towhead like his mom. The first time Bob left for two weeks in the field, he came home, and Seth wouldn't go to him. You could see it really crushed Bob. And now he'll be gone six months. He's seen kids hide from their dads when they return from a float; he's seen kids cower in fear. And Luke, her son by her first marriage, has grown close to Bob as well. Luke likes to tell the story of how Bob took him fishing for the first time. Luke caught a catfish that was *this* long. Actually, Bob helped. "But he told everyone I caught it myself," Luke says proudly.

With everyone out of the house for a while, Sinclair is taking some time to reflect, a little reluctantly, on his career. He rocks back and forth gently in his chair. "This is probably going to sound like propaganda," he says, taking the opportunity, in his family's absence, to indulge himself in a dip, "but my primary motivation for being a Marine is that I love this country. I feel that being born in this country is a privilege. Right, wrong, or indifferent, this is still the greatest country in the world. All you have to do is travel to figure that one out. I thank the good Lord that we have a lot of great men and women in this country who feel the same way as I feel, who are willing to make that ultimate sacrifice for what they believe in. None of us wants to die. But we know if we have to, it's for the greatest reasons.

"I have to admit that becoming a dad, especially this late in life, has completely changed me. When you're younger, it was like, *Okay, if you die, you can leave your parents behind, or your brothers. That* would be sad, but you know, you can kind of accept that. Once you get married, you're kinda like, *Hmmm*. But you can justify that, too. The wife's an adult, she's intelligent, she's beautiful, she can get on with life. But then all of a sudden, you've got that child. I never understood it until Seth was born and lying there in the hospital weighing two pounds, not knowing whether he was going to live or die. And I just looked at him and said, 'This is a life that we've created and that I'm responsible for.' His entire hand could grab around the knuckle of my little finger when he squeezed."

He rocks in his chair; he is a man who is seldom at rest, who wakes up at full speed and doesn't stop until he shuts his eyes, whereupon he falls instantly into a deep untroubled sleep, as he did on the couch after the FEX, on the night of his anniversary. At least he made it through dinner.

Birds sing in the trees. A lawn mower drones, echoing through the cul-de-sac. The grass in his backyard is lush and green; the fence line is planted with riotous bougainvillea, rich shades of red and purple and pink. An old dog naps at his feet. A small fountain gurgles at the back corner of the lot. "I know this float is going to be tough," Sinclair says. "But it's like anything else. We'll get on that ship, we'll do what we have to do, and then we'll come back, and life will continue to move on. That'll be six months you can never make up, but what we do as Marines is that important. Nobody wrenches your arm to sign that contract. These men do this on their own. They all know the risks. That's why leading them is just an honor beyond belief.

"I am loyal to the Corps, but my family is more important to me. If you take it in order, I'd say it's God, country, family, and then way down at number four on the list is the Marine Corps. That's not insulting the Corps; it's just that the bottom line is that someday the Corps is gonna kick every one of us out. Even the commandant of the Marine Corps is gonna retire, and they're gonna say, 'Thank you very much for all your years of service, General, but it's time to move on.' They're gonna do the same to me. They always say we're here to train our own replacements. There will always be plenty of great people to take my place. But my family will always be there for me. I mean, I'll probably be up for colonel soon. But with our family situation—the fact that, you know, Jessie can't leave the state to share custody of Luke..." His voice trails off. "I'd hate to leave the Corps, but I can't leave my family and become a geographical bachelor again."

He spits a stream of brownish juice onto the lawn. "The bottom line comes down to this: It's hard to put into words. It's more like a feeling. You feel it, and you know it's right. It's like trying to explain morals or religion or love. The Marine Corps exists to fight and win America's battles, to help keep our country free. It sounds corny, I suppose. But like they say, somebody's got to do it. I guess one of those somebodies is me."

***

September 2001: Sinclair is at his desk at Camp Horno. There is a heightened security aboard the base, but training continues as normal. Sinclair's deuce gear and his flak vest and his helmet lie in a heap in the corner of the small room. His M9 sidearm, holstered, is atop his desk.

On September 11, upon waking to the horrific news from the East Coast, Sinclair called his XO, Major Weede, and told him he was going to stay put for a while and watch the events unfold on television. He felt a need to be home with his family. He also knew he didn't have to hurry to the base; it takes a long time to plan military action, Sinclair points out. The Japanese bombed Pearl Harbor on December 7, 1941. The first ground offensive by U.S. forces against the Japanese didn't occur until August 7, 1942, when the 1st Marine Division—the division that includes Sinclair's One-Four—invaded Guadalcanal.

Come January, however, or whenever Sinclair and his 13th MEU (SOC) steam out into the WestPac, things will probably be much different. The kind of campaign they're talking about is the kind the One-Four has been trained to undertake. With the threat of war, perhaps a sustained one, Bob and Jessie Sinclair must put their worries about career and future and geographical bachelorhood aside. There is no doubt about the order of his priorities at a time like this.

"It's one of those things where you train your whole life for something you hope you never actually have to execute. But I think there's something primal about each one of us Marines. If we're at war, you want to be in the operating forces. You don't want to be sitting on the sidelines. This is what we do. This is what we're trained for.

"The initial thing I felt, seeing that plane fly into the tower, seeing the pictures of the Pentagon, was absolute anger. You realize that your country has been attacked. That is a deep, deep wound, a sharp slap to the face. You wanna strike back. But at the same time, you have to keep your head. You know that you've got this whole system in place. There are politicians and diplomats. In a way, you're angry deep down inside your gut, but you're also in realization that, okay, there are people who are much smarter than me, and they are in charge, and I completely trust their leadership. As a member of the military, I'm here to support and implement whatever decision they make.

"Like the president said, 'Get ready.' Well, we are ready. This battalion is ready right now. We'll do what needs to be done."

Wounded Warriors

Meet Ringo, Wildman, Sergeant D, Lieutenant
Colonel Maxwell, and the rest of the Devil Dogs
at the Wounded Warrior Barracks at Camp
Lejeune, North Carolina. From day one, the
Marine Corps trained them to be lean, mean
killing machines. But what happens after the
machine is broken? A report on the wars in
Afghanistan and Iraq and the human aftermath.

Ringo and Wildman are kickin' it with Jo-Jo, Hazy, Sergeant D,
and the rest of the Devil Dogs in the rec room at Maxwell Hall
when who should come through the hatch but the old man himself,
Lieutenant Colonel Tim Maxwell, the guy for whom the barracks
was named.

Thick-shouldered and squared away, Maxwell is dressed
in his digital cammies—the sleeves of his tunic rolled cleanly to
his biceps, the trouser cuffs banded securely around the shanks
of his sand-colored suede combat boots—the uniform of the day
aboard Camp Lejeune, North Carolina. Forty-two years old with
nineteen years in (twenty-three if you count ROTC), Maxwell did
five deployments overseas without a scratch. Then one afternoon
in 2004, three months into his sixth, in the southern Iraqi town of
Kalsu, he decided to take a power nap—fifteen minutes after chow.
He'd heard about it somewhere: Many leaders through history had
done the same—a short pause to refresh.

Now he pauses just inside the door of Maxwell Hall and looks around, smiling his slightly crooked smile. The right side of his face still lags; it might come back, or it might not—there is no way to predict. The room has been recently repainted, the windows replaced. The new carpet is due soon; the workmen have moved on to the fitness center next door. It is July. Outside, the temperature and the humidity are both in the high 90s. Tree frogs bark, cicadas sing their familiar summer song in the lush and tangled undergrowth. In here it is air-conditioned, a cool 69 degrees. A couple dozen enlisted men and NCOs are hanging out—shooting eight ball, playing Call of Duty on the new Xbox 360, watching a cable movie on the big flat-screen TV. One group is huddled together on the doctor's-office-variety chairs, talking smack, scratching, waiting for pizzas to be delivered so they can eat their afternoon pain meds, which need to be taken with food. (The chow hall is just across the way. Nobody eats there, even though the cost of meals is deducted from their pay, which runs about $1,700 a month for a corporal, $1,300 for a private.) A couple of the guys are racked out on the new leather sofas. One kid with his mouth wide open is snoring loud enough to interrupt the dialog of the movie, *Risky Business*, about the hijinks of carefree high school boys in the affluent suburbs. Two more guys luxuriate in massage chairs, fancy models like something from Sharper Image, the hum of which is clearly audible beneath the raucous, clubhouse din generated by this assembly of young men, most of them in their late teens and early twenties, most of them damaged beyond full repair. In conversation, Maxwell fondly calls them "my Marines." He has a thickish Southern drawl that he picked up from some mysterious recess of his brain when he began to recover his speech after the injury. In fact, he was born in Ohio.

Maxwell spots the guy he's looking for and moves in that direction, his gait powerful but uneven, like Chesty the bulldog with a limp. He has a strong jaw and piercing blue eyes; there is a large scar on the left side of his head, a ropey pink question mark that runs like concertina wire below the hedge line of his high-and-tight military flattop. He has trouble reading and taking instructions. His short-term memory is shot. It took him forever to build the little fort in the backyard for his son; he had to keep rereading each step of the directions over and over again. He tells his daughter to put refrigerator on her tuna sandwich. He refers to the airport as "the place where people come to fly," and to Somalia, where he once served, as "that country in Africa." His hernia, which he kept a painful secret so as not to miss his final deployment, is "that problem with your nuts." He calls the family's new dog Magic instead of Miracle (though he can remember perfectly the name of their old dog, Bella). His right arm and right leg are functional but "clumpy." He can still run several miles on a treadmill; he does three sets of ten bicep curls, thirty-five pounds each.

Though his IQ, his reflexes, his limb strength, all of his measurable functions are down from their "factory of original," as he likes to put it, he is still within what doctors tell him are "acceptable ranges." *Acceptable to whom?* Maxwell wonders. He will never be the same. He will never be as good. It weighs on him, you can tell. He is the type of man who has spent his whole life pushing and striving, trying to raise his score or to lower his time, a man who never took the easy path: As a high school kid, he wanted to play lineman in football, even though he weighed only 140 pounds. He took his undergrad degree in engineering and a masters in statistics, even though he struggled with math. He eats "morale" pills (he tried four varieties before settling on Effexor), anti-seizure pills (five varieties), more pills every day than he is capable of recalling. All the pills have side effects. Here is the list for Effexor: constipation, dizziness, dry mouth, insomnia, loss of appetite, nausea, nervousness, sexual side effects, sleepiness, sweating, and weakness. Ask your doctor if Effexor may be right for you. Ooh-rah. Sometimes, his brain starts to crash. That is his word for it. His speech becomes slurry; he gets this look on his face like a guy who has been up for several days doing alcohol and drugs. He just has to shut it all down and go to bed. It happened earlier this week, after he drove the six hours in his old green Land Rover to Quantico, Virginia, to meet his new boss. He is still on active duty. He's due to report to his new billet in one week.

Corporal Justin Kinnee is sitting on one of the sofas, staring at the flat-screen through a pair of dark Nike sport sunglasses, the kind issued to troops in Iraq. Several of the guys in the room are wearing them. Extreme sensitivity to light can be one of the symptoms of a traumatic brain injury (TBI). Dilated pupils, another cause of light sensitivity, can also be a side effect of some prescription drugs. In previous U.S. military conflicts, 14 to 20 percent of surviving casualties reportedly suffered TBIs. Of the 28,000 American troops injured so far in Iraq, anywhere from a quarter to a half are estimated to have suffered TBIs. Another statistic: The Marine Corps, which is the smallest of all the U.S. armed forces, has sustained nearly one-third of all the casualties in Iraq, due to assignments in sectors like the Anbar Province, the heart of the Sunni insurgency and the deadliest place in Iraq for U.S. troops thus far in the war. In bygone days, after you got whacked, the Marine Corps gave you a Purple Heart—the medal that no Marine wants—and a discharge. Then, they sent you on your way to deal with the Veterans Administration for the rest of your life. Now, due to Maxwell's efforts, there is not only a barracks for wounded warriors aboard Camp Lejeune (and another aboard Camp Pendleton in California), but there is also a brand-new Wounded Warrior Regiment in the Marine Corps. That's why Maxwell is moving—he's joining the general staff as an advisor. Though none of the men know it yet, this is his last day in Maxwell Hall.

Before he enlisted, Kinnee was a sheriff's deputy in Cherokee County, Georgia. He'd been in Iraq three months when a piece of shrapnel ripped open his neck. He lost five of his six quarts of blood, stroked out, died in the dust. Somehow, they saved him. There is a precise-looking scar on his head, just right of center—running from the front hairline to the back, like a part scissored into his crew cut, which he has trimmed for seven dollars every Sunday after church—where they removed a portion of his skull to allow his brain to swell after the stroke. Now he has an acrylic plate and twenty screws—"five screws per manhole cover," he likes to say; you can feel where the plate starts. As a result of the stroke, his left arm doesn't work. He takes special meds to keep it from becoming palsied; at night, he sleeps with a brace on his hand. After he sits down, he will typically use his right hand to reach over and pick up his left arm by the wrist and place it on his lap, this inert thing attached to him that must be managed.

"How you doin', Kinnee?" Maxwell asks. He cops a lean on the arm of the sofa opposite and crosses his arms.

Kinnee looks up, groggy at first, uninterested. Then he realizes who's in front of him and snaps to a seated form of attention. Though he can't fully dress himself without help (the fussy rolled cuffs and trousers ties, the calf-high lace-up boots; "try putting on a sock with one hand," he says in his typical challenging tone, the result of personality changes and disinhibition caused by the death of the right hemisphere of his brain) he is one of the more motivated Marines in Maxwell Hall, at least when it comes to doing chores and maintaining military discipline. Having joined later in life than most of the guys, Kinnee, twenty-six, is more serious. He made corporal in only two years. This was going to be a career for him.

"Fine and dandy, sir," Kinnee answers dryly. There is a cast to his face, a waxen awkwardness, as if the left side and the right side are expressing different emotions simultaneously. Think of your mouth after dental surgery. He always carries tissues or a napkin to mop up any moisture. Kinnee's tongue is tricky, too, as is Maxwell's. The words come out with some difficulty.

"Did you start that morale pill we talked about?" Maxwell asks. "That shit is *intense.*"

A puzzled expression: "How so, sir?"

"How much did the doc give you per day?"

"I'm not sure. I told him what we talked about. How I was concerned, you know, about how my brother was saying I seemed to be more short-tempered than before. I got some concern that I don't wanna change too much or I'll push everybody away."

"Give yourself about two, three weeks," Maxwell advises. "After that, if you don't like the side effects, or if you think it's making you feel too weird or whatever, go back to that fuckin' doctor and get yourself another kind. I had to try a few different kinds before I got this one, I can't remember the frickin' name—my wife told you, right? Temper is what they started giving it to me for a long time ago, actually. So give it a shot. But don't expect a miracle."

"I'll try, sir."

Maxwell regards him a moment, sizing him up the way a mother might take measure of her child at the end of a long school day. "Your morale seems better," he says. "That trip home musta did you good. Did you get that ball for your hand?"

"No, sir."

Maxwell thumps the corporal playfully on the shoulder. "Come on, *man*." Before he was injured, Kinnee was bench-pressing 225 pounds. He carried heavy field radio equipment. He studies his boots.

"How much does it work?" Maxwell asks, his tone bright and encouraging.

Looking up: "What?"

"The arm. How much does it work? Does it have *some* utility?"

"I can squeeze the hand shut but I can't open it," Kinnee says. He doesn't bother to demonstrate.

"Fuckin' brain injuries," Maxwell says, shaking his head. "You know that, um—what's that chubby kid's name?"

"Reynolds?"

"Reynolds," Maxwell repeats, tapping the front of his broad forehead with his fingertip. "Reynolds. Reynolds. Before I leave, I have to go around and get everyone's picture and label them. I can't remember anyone's frickin' name."

"I can only remember what I knew before, sir," Kinnee concurs.

"Anyway, *R-R-Reynolds*," Maxwell says, struggling with the name, his jaw working awkwardly on its hinge like a man with a bad stutter. "*R-Reynolds'* hand didn't work at all, and his leg didn't work. But look at him now. He got a lot of it back."

"We'll see," Kinnee says, not at all convinced. In the images he's seen of his brain, the left side is entirely white, and the right side is entirely black. "That means it's dead," he'll explain later.

Maxwell searches the ceiling for a lighter topic. In earlier phases of his military career, he often found himself out among the troops, polling them, taking stock, reporting back to superiors.

He likes to see himself as an idea man, as a guy who understands a little bit about what people need. Like the day he came across that young Devil Dog alone in his barracks, crying. The rest of his unit was still in Iraq. This boy was back at home, injured and alone, fighting his own fight, trying to recover. Wounds in combat are not like the ones in the movies. You hear about the amputees, the burn guys. But one bullet through the arm can turn a bone to sand. The nerve damage creates pain enough to make a junkie. The limb will never be right again. From day one in training, they teach a Marine that there's no *I* in *team*. They teach him that he's only as good as the man on his left and the man on his right. They teach him to be a lean, mean killing machine. What happens after the machine is broken?

So it was that Maxwell took his idea up the chain of command. He was assisted by his wife, Shannon, who had started a support group for Marine families, and by Thomas Barraga, a former Marine and a local legislator in Suffolk County, New York, who worked with Maxwell to write a proposal for a "medical rehabilitation platoon." Within fourteen months of Maxwell's injury, by order of Lieutenant General James F. Amos, then commanding general of the 2nd Marine Expeditionary Force, there was a new central billet for injured Marines. Maxwell Hall was open.

Maxwell checks his watch. His arm rotates awkwardly; he also took shrapnel to his left elbow. "A'ight," he drawls, "I gotta get going to the next item on my checkout list. I'm almost done. I gotta go to the C, uh"—he stumbles over the initials—"CSI."

"What's that, sir?"

Maxwell thinks a moment. "Oh. *CSI* is a movie. About cops."

"You mean, frickin', uh—" Kinnee gestures in the air with his hand, pointing generally to the west.

"*Yeah*. You know. The, uh—" an open palm, wrist rotating in the same direction.

Nodding conclusively: "Yeah."

"That's right."

"Okay, then. Catch you later."

**

I'm Justin Kinnee, I'm twenty-six. This is my room in Maxwell Hall. It ain't nothin' special. It's where I live for right now. I was originally born in Pasadena, California. I stayed there until I was fourteen. We moved around a lot. My mother was a single mom with two boys. Eventually we ended up in Georgia, just north of Atlanta.

The right side of my brain doesn't work at all. You use your whole brain; I'm using half of mine. Stuff I knew before the injury, births and dates and stuff like that, I can still tell you. Everything after the injury is a little fuzzy. Like I can't remember names. The only way I can remember your first name is because it's my middle name. Justin Michael Kinnee. Your name is Michael, so I can remember it.

Memory is a game that's played every day. It's just a developing thing. I mean, I'm not speaking as well as I was a few months ago. By doing the exercises that I was taught, I'm trying to get better. The part of my brain that works the best is vision. Like, the medicines I take? I know which one to take because I know the color. I know that the white pill and the red-and-white pill are both my sleeping medicines. I know the yellow pill is for my seizures, and so on and so forth. After the injury that's how my brain works. I know the colors of the medicines, but I don't know the names. I just know what they're for and what color they are. I take a lot of pills. Here they are in this box on my shelf. This is a pain pill, this is a pain pill, this is a pain pill. Sleeping, sleeping, sleeping, sleeping—oh sorry, this is a nerve pill, *that* one is for sleeping. Seizure medicine, multivitamin, tone medicine. T-O-N-E. Like muscle tone. See, since my left arm doesn't work, what happens is your body tends to kind of want to do this, you know, your fingers and your limbs want to curl up. You see it with paralyzed people all the time. The drug keeps it relaxed. Right now, if I wasn't taking the drug, my arm would be all curled up, which would put strain on the muscles and nerves and everything else. The medicine allows it to relax. Plus, I wear a brace at night that keeps my fingers straight, because night is the worst time for that to happen—night is when you grow and you heal; when your brain shuts down, your body reacts to that. So if I wasn't wearing that brace and I wasn't taking that medicine, then my hand, when it came back to its full use, would be like this (he makes a palsied claw with his good hand). That is, if it ever does come back.

In October of this year, it'll be two years. It has gotten a little better. My improvement has gone up, but it has also kind of hit a plateau. When I first got here, I couldn't do a lot of shoulder movements. Now I can do some shrugs. And there's this exercise where I have to sit up on my elbows. I couldn't do that before—I couldn't hold it—but now I can. You have to understand: I was huge before I got hurt. I was about 160 pounds. I'm only five ten. I was just massive. In Iraq, I was benching 225 plus. When you're in my job, infantry, that's all you do. That's your whole job. You work out, you run, you tone up. If I'm not in shape and somebody gets shot or something, and I can't pick them up and carry them away, then I just killed that Marine for no reason. I took it as a personal responsibility to make sure I was in the absolute best shape I could be in. That way I could handle everything. Plus, we were wearing, frickin', a hundred pounds of gear. And then I wore extra 'cause I was the radio guy, so I had the radio and the antenna and the batteries. It's a lot extra. Fifty pounds at least. Extra weight and extra responsibility. That's an important job. I'm not tootin' my own horn, but they don't just throw anybody on that.

I joined in August, 2004, when I was twenty-two. I'd been to junior college for two years. I'd been a cop for a year. I remember being an only child in the beginning, before my brother was born. There was no one to play with, so I always played with those little green plastic soldiers. I don't know why: being a Marine was just something I've always wanted to do. By the time I joined, it was sorta like now or never. I was getting a little old. The war was going on in Iraq. I felt like I needed to do something to help. Now I been in almost three years. It's been incredible. I really love it.

The main thing is, I got in because I wanted to make a difference. That's why I picked the infantry. I didn't just wanna hear about the war from somewhere back in the rear, I wanted to be up front and be able to say, 'This is what really happened.' I wanted to really be able to make a difference. I wanted to be the best Marine I could be—one of the ones making the most difference. This was my first pump. I was in the Two-Six. I was only there for three months and one week; I was injured on the eighth day of October, 2005. That's what it says on my Purple Heart. We were in Fallujah, so we were right between Baghdad and the Syrian border, which is not such a great spot to be in, because everything and everybody comes in through the Syrian border to try to get to Baghdad. We were standing in between 'em. There was just constant stuff every day.

See, you got three units in the battalion. My unit was Fox Company— about 600 Marines. My unit alone captured three Al Qaeda members off the FBI's blacklist. But you'll never hear that on TV, because that's a positive note of why we're there fighting and doing our jobs over there. On the news, you only hear the crap—we got blown up, or somebody died, or we killed somebody. Another thing you never hear is, well... lemme tell you this story, see what you think.

One day, I was on post. We'd occupied this house on a street somewhere and we were standing watch. That's really what we do a lot of there. We're like police. We hunt down wanted persons, answer to problems among the citizenry, watch for the enemy, patrol, stand post. And we have the Iraqi Army with us—we're supposed to be training them to do all those things. So I'm on post on this roof, and I'm looking out. Over in the distance, we've got three lines—a green, a yellow, and a red line. Well, there's not exactly a line *per se*; there are these markers made of wood, set at intervals of one hundred meters, usually. The first is green, the second is yellow, the third is red—red being the one that gets you killed. If Joe Blow Muhammad Ali, whatever you wanna call him, crosses the green line, you sound a blow horn. If he passes the yellow line, maybe you set off a flash bang. If they cross the red line, you have to shoot 'em because at that point, if they do have an explosive device and they detonate it, everybody would die. So that's the scene. One day, I was on post, and there was this kid. He was playing with a ball.

And he kept crossing the first two lines, the green and the yellow. When he did that, we had to blow the horn, we had to set off a flash bang. But he just kept going back and forth, playing with his ball, a basketball, bouncing it up and down, not even paying any attention to us. And the thing was, there was this bush, see. This bush by the side of a house. And sometimes the kid would go behind the bush, you know, disappear from my sight. I couldn't really see where he was going, because the bush was in the way.

Long story short: One time, the ball came rolling out past all three lines, all the way to our barbed wire—*way* across the red line. This kid couldn't have been but six years old. Now like I said, I was a cop before I joined the Marine Corps. I'm thinking, *This is a little suspicious.* Before he was bouncing the ball but now, all of a sudden, at this point in time, the ball's rolling all the way to our wire. Why would the kid roll the ball all the way past the line? I gotta juggle all these things in my mind, and now I gotta think—I gotta make a split-second decision. If I kill this kid, I gotta live with that for the rest of my life. If I don't, I could possibly kill twenty Marines.

Turned out, the kid was wired with a bomb. It was perfectly orchestrated. We called the QRF, which is quick reaction force. They come, and apparently, what I couldn't see, behind that bush was the kid's father. He was taking pictures of his child with a video camera. That bastard was just waiting for me to kill the kid, his own flesh and blood, so he could film it and to put it on their Muhammad Ali TV to make us look even worse over there in the A-rab world. And then they could sell that for money to CNN and all this crap, and we would just look like total shitheads. You'll never hear that shit on TV, you'll just hear what bastards we are over there. How we are murderers and all this shit. I mean, there wasn't no draft. We volunteered to do this job for not much pay. You know, we're not makin' a hundred grand a year over there. I'm making less than thirty and I'm twenty-six years old. Less than thirty grand to go over there and have my legs blown off, or die, or live on machines the rest of my life. I'm there to do a job. We're there to do a job. And we get nothing but bullshit on the TV news. That's something for you to think about.

The day before my injury, we had a twelve-hour patrol. We have a twelve-man squad, and we patrol the city after curfew. We're on foot. I'm carrying 150 pounds, including the field radio. After twelve hours, we come back to post. We're exhausted as hell. We're sweating our asses off, which sucks because over there it's 130 degrees every day, but as soon as night hits it gets freezing-ass cold, and all of a sudden your balls are freezing, because you've been sweating all day, but now it's cold, and everything's wet at that point, and then you're just frickin' miserable. After the patrol, we come back to stand post, which means another eight to ten hours when we're back in our FOB (forward operating base, pronounced like Bob) standing security, in case insurgents attack. So that's how our rotation works. After patrol, we went to the post, and after the post we went to bed, which was great. Frickin' sleep. Oh God! That's the best sleep. 'Cause you don't have to think about sleepin', you know? As soon as you take off your clothes—I change into clean clothes because I didn't want to sleep wet—I change into clean clothes, and *boom*, I'm gone, I'm out like a light, that's all she wrote. Then you had to wake up like eight hours later and *boom*, you know, we get the call, we're back on patrol again.

That day was weird. That morning I'd gotten a modem mail from my fiancée at the time. Modem mail is like email. Your family or friends can send you emails, and it comes to you on paper, like a telegram. Like a letter, you know. So instead of waiting for a week for the mail, it's instant. It's really great. So I got a modem mail from my fiancée at the time. My ex-fiancée. We'd broke up before I left, but in this mail, she said she wanted to get back together, so that was kind of a good thing. I put that modem mail in my pocket, grabbed my iPod, got dressed. Then we left.

We couldn't have gone but one hundred yards out of the FOB. We turned the corner to go down the alley, headed toward the city itself. I was in the middle of the formation because I had to stay with the squad leader—he's the one with the GPS (global positioning system, like those things you can get now for your cars, only a military version). One of my jobs is to walk with him and report our Pos Ref, position reference. He gives me the GPS coordinates and I call them into headquarters, and they put a pin where we are on the map, so if some shit went down, they would know where our last coordinates were. So we're walking, and the fire team ahead of us went past this open field. And then we came along. When you're at war, the two things that any military in the world will hit first are your com, your communications, and your machine gunner. And that's exactly what happened to me. The fire team was allowed to pass by the initial point where the IED, improvised explosive device, was hidden—this place in the open field. I remember, I had just did a Pos Ref, and then I hung up the radio. And then we came up on that point. And that's when it happened—*Boom!* It was two feet away from me on my right side.

I woke up on the ground. I was like, *Shit*. I felt like I'd got hit by a damn fucking truck. There was blood everywhere. My neck was ripped open. See here on my neck? My little happy face made out of scars? It wasn't that happy at that time. My whole neck was ripped open. I can't feel it to point it to you—I have no feeling in my neck anymore. But see right here? Right where my throat is? Below my Adams apple? There was a big hole there. All of the air in my lungs was coming out of it. The artery, the carotid artery—it's right in there, too. It was ripped open. Every time my heart would pump, it would pump the blood straight out of my body. The doctors said that everybody has six quarts of blood. I lost five. No blood. No air. *Boom*: You stroke out. You die. I have no idea how they saved my sorry ass. Those docs are the best in the world.

When you have a stroke, your brain swells. They had to cut this chunk out of my skull, so my brain would have somewhere to go. Now I have this acrylic plate. On a CAT scan, everybody's brain is supposed to look white. If you have a tumor or something, you'd have a black spot. The CAT scan of my brain shows one white half and one black half. By medical terms, half my brain is literally dead—it just doesn't work. Which is why this arm, my left, doesn't work, because the signals that come from that side of the brain aren't there. They're dead, they're gone, they're *fried*. Now, the left side of my brain, my right, has to take over. At first, I couldn't speak, I couldn't swallow, I couldn't talk. I still can't feel my face.

It's like you've just been to the dentist, only it's permanent. When I eat, I usually have a lot of napkins just to wipe. It's a habit now, because I'll have a piece of food hanging there if I don't watch it. Sometimes I drool. If I've got something on my face, you need to tell me about it. Sometimes it gets all crazy over there.

I'm not mad or angry. I don't regret any of it. I am a little frustrated. I get frustrated easier now, for sure. My brother says I'm more short-tempered, but that's nothing I can control. Emotion is on the side of my brain that's dead. It's just something you have to work through every day, to try to get better. The biggest problem is there's not much I can do. Can't play pool or video games or fish, can't run, can't ride a bike, can't PT, can't do shit. I can watch a movie as long as the plot is not too involved. I can read. It's not so good, but I can read. I wear glasses—I lost vision in both eyes. I can see peripheral vision on my right, but I have none on my left. I had to go through a lot of classes to be able to be cleared to drive. I have to wear glasses, and I have to do a lot of scanning to make sure I see stuff coming on the left side. The reason I wear the sunglasses inside is because my brain doesn't know how to interpret the lighting inside. Like, the sun's okay—not too much of it, but it's okay, because it's a natural thing, and my eyes are a natural thing, or so they tell me. But not the man-made light. Weird, isn't it? You find out a lot of weird things about yourself in this process, weird quirks of the human body that you have absolutely no control over.

What plans do I have for the future? Well, in the immediate future there is another operation on my knee. I didn't tell you—in the IED explosion, my legs snapped, too, like a pencil. Since the IED was so close, I'm fortunate to still have the legs. See, you've got me with my 150 pounds of stuff on my back standing straight up like this, and gravity holding you down. And all of a sudden, this massive force just hits you on the side. Snap, just like two pencils. But anyways, the future—after the surgery and all the therapy and that whole thing? To be honest with you, I'm looking at options. I'm a man of faith. The way I look at it is this: The Lord could have killed me. He coulda let me die right there. I mean, I did die. My heart stopped, I bled out almost all my blood. But he didn't take me

He let me live. So there's a reason why I'm here. There's a reason why I'm alive. I don't know what that reason is. I don't know what I'm doing. But he got me to this point, so he's just gonna have to open the door for me when I get wherever it is that I'm going. I'm gonna do what I think is right, but as far as, like, going to law school or medical school or some other crazy shit, I don't really have a big plan. The Marine Corps was my Plan A. I didn't have no plan B. This was my Plan A, B, and C. This was it. But life doesn't always work out the way you want, you know what I'm sayin'? I'm like, 'Okay, I can do this, I can overcome.' I got no other choice.

***

Ten in the morning on the second floor of Maxwell Hall. Four guys are hanging out in somebody's room, call him Lance Corporal Romeo. It could be a college dorm, a double suite with connecting bath, each side eight by twelve with full cable hookup. You can pay extra for Internet.

Leeman and Ringo are on the sofa, using Romeo's laptop, YouTubing videos from Iraq of IED explosions and firefights; one of their favorites is set to the song "American Idiot." Cybula is on a folding chair, poking through the small fridge—nobody's had shit to eat today. You have to be up and dressed to report for formation at 7:00 a.m. Then... nothing. A few guys have jobs or duties. These four do not. Romeo is on the queen-size bed, which faces a big-screen television. It has a built-in DVD player, standard issue in every room. On top of the TV are an Xbox and a PS2, two of the dozens of donated gaming systems floating around Maxwell Hall. All of the components fit snugly into a cherrywood armoire/entertainment center, also standard issue. Next to him on the bed is a beautiful young girl with flame-red hair and freckles, a rising senior at a high school twenty miles away. She says she's eighteen. Romeo met her a couple of weeks ago at a stoplight. Of all the Marines in town— there would hardly be a reason for Jacksonville if there were no Marines; they are everywhere in this franchise heaven of a city, looking as uniform in their civvies as they do in their uniforms:

cargo shorts, Nikes, t-shirt, baseball cap optional—for some reason she settled on him. She visits regularly, often in the evenings. If he asks, she'll bring a pizza. Once, in the middle of sex with her, his wife called. He picked up his cell phone and proceeded to have a conversation. At the moment, the redhead is transfixed on the TV screen, pressing buttons on a toy guitar, a video game she is playing. Nobody pays her any mind.

"I miss Iraq so bad," Leeman says, clicking on another YouTube selection. Corporal Jeff Leeman is the ranking NCO in the room. He is tall and thin, twenty years old, from Lebanon, Tennessee. He talks low and fast and swallows his words like Boomhauer on *King of the Hill*.

"I know, man. *Fuck!* I just wanna kill some of those fuckin' people." This is Ringo, Lance Corporal Jeremy Dru Ringgold, twenty-two. He has big blue eyes and the gift of gab, an accent like the Marlboro man. He seems especially upbeat today, loud and expressive, a little bit hype.

"Watch this'n," Leeman mumbles. "Suicide bomber. Black car right thar. He's approachin' a checkpoint. Wait for it..."

Boooooom!

The small extension speakers on the coffee table shake and rattle and hiss.

"Ohhhhh, shit!"

"Fuuuuuck!"

"That's *horrible*, dude."

"There's this one video I wish I could find," Ringo says, grabbing the keyboard away from Leeman. "It has this Iraqi. He's in his car sitting next to all these 155 shells. He's fuckin', like, petting the fuckin' things. And then he drives down the road and blows himself up. I'm like, What the fuck, man? Why didn't you come to me and let me shoot you in the fuckin' face?"

A native of Augusta, Georgia, Ringo is charismatic, intelligent, and well liked. Lately, he has developed a potbelly from lack of exercise and too much beer, which he shouldn't be drinking anyway, due to his regular use of Percocet, which helps to mask the excruciating nerve pain in his arm. As a side effect of the drug, he is constantly rubbing his nose and sniffling— his behavior and the tone of his voice are very much reminiscent of a heroin addict. In fact, he says his brother was a heroin addict. His sister got pregnant and left home at fifteen. His other brother is a Marine. Like every other Marine in the room (and all but one of the Marines I met at Maxwell Hall, including Maxwell himself), Ringo is a child of divorce. He didn't know his father very well. He does remember that his father gave him his first rifle, an AR-15, when he was nine. Until recently, to help pass the great stretches of unoccupied time as he endures the Middle Passage of the healing process, Ringo was working as a teacher's aide in an elementary school not far from base. Now that school is out, he says he's "bored outta my fuckin' mind." Back home, Ringo's wife, whom he calls Skinny (his screen name is *Skeremy*), is living in the house he recently bought for $90,000—his offer despite the asking price of $150,000. ("My wife and the agent thought I was crazy, but hey—that's all I could afford.") He has not yet slept there. She is a manager at a grocery store, pregnant with their first child, a little girl; he realizes he might end up having to shoot some guy someday for trying to get fresh—ha, ha, just kidding, he says.

Ringo did two tours in Iraq. During his first, he lost half his squad to a suicide car bomber. During his second, twenty-two days in, he got hit—trying to save a Marine he'd never met before. He didn't even have to be on that patrol; for some crazy reason, he'd volunteered to sub in with another squad. At the top of the firefight, he got hit in the helmet—it went clear through but never touched his scalp. Then a second bullet found his forearm and turned it into chips and dust. He is convinced he was supposed to die that day. He doesn't know why he didn't. He feels guilty for getting injured. He was a team leader. After he left, some of his Marines got whacked. Maybe if he had been there...

Cybula burps loudly, causing everyone to laugh. Lance Corporal John Cybula, twenty-one, is a handsome guy from Sweetwater, Tennessee, raised by his grandparents. The top of his hair is a little longer than regulation; it's all gussied up with gel. He can sit at a table in a burger joint with two friends, and before he leaves, a cute little female Marine, short-time to deployment, will give him her number. After he got whacked, Cybula ended up marrying his nurse from the hospital in Portsmouth, Virginia. She's still up there. She wants a divorce. He just discovered that she cleaned out his bank account. He has four one-dollar bills to his name— another explanation for his hunger. Reaching into a shelf, he pulls out a bag of Romeo's extra-spicy style Doritos. He rips it open, begins stuffing his face.

"I'll tell you something," Ringo says, standing up now, pacing the room energetically, two steps forward, turn, two steps back. "The first time I held a rifle in my hand and realized it made shit blow up, I was like, 'You know what? This is what life is all about right here.'"

"I heard *dat*," Leeman says, taking back the laptop. Almost all of the guys have deep caches of digital photos and homemade videos of themselves and their tours. Often, during a firefight, guys can be seen shooting videos. The most searing image I saw was a digital photo of the face of a suicide bomber a few moments *after* a blast— just the face, disembodied, lying abandoned in the street, as if the forehead and nose and mouth had been removed to be used as a Halloween mask.

Cybula burps again, theatrically, enjoying the attention of the group. He was on the roof of a building when a sniper bullet caught him in the back of his flak vest and knocked him through a hole. He fell three stories, broke his knee and pelvis. The Marines are not convinced about the sniper part of the story; his Purple Heart has thus far been denied. Cybula is on morphine and Vicodin. He's also on meds to help him sleep and meds to block his dreams. He says he can't sleep without getting drunk, which he does many nights— beer and shots. His eyes are slits. His body itches all over from the morphine; he's constantly scratching. Back when he was on Demerol, only his stomach itched. Now it's everywhere, usually just out of reach. He has a sly smile, a sweet vibe that kills the ladies; you can tell there's a really nice guy buried somewhere inside all of that medication.

Ringo and Cybula used to be suitemates, but then Ringo was ordered to move to another barracks because of the overflow. He had been in Maxwell Hall for nearly six months. He hates his new barracks. It's a pog barracks, which stands for "person other than grunt," meaning someone who is not in the infantry. Pogs are lower than the skin on a snake's belly, lower than a hemorrhoid on a Haji's ass, etc. Leeman is a pog because he rides in a pussy LAV, a light-armored vehicle, instead of humping like the real men. Lucky for Leeman, they take pity on his pog self and let him hang around. As fate would have it, he outranks them. Presumably, pogs have more time to study for advancement exams. Ringo's pog barracks, which is full of administrative personnel—*super*pogs—is quiet and sterile. These weird, big bugs from the marsh crawl under the door and into his room. There is no TV or pool table or Sharper Image massaging chair, and nobody else who has ever been in a firefight, much less been wounded in one. Lately he's been staying at Maxwell Hall, sleeping in the queen-size bed with Cybula.

"Did I tell you what happened last night?" Ringo asks, super-animated, still pacing.

"That was one helluva storm," Leeman says. "My dogs was goin' crazy."

Leeman was on his first tour when the eight-wheeled armored wagon he was driving hit a pressure-plate mine. They were only about 500 meters outside the gate of their FOB. He was able to call in his own three-line injury report over the radio before everything went black, he explains with mumbled bravado. Because he doesn't have a fake ID, Leeman—who will not turn twenty-one for a couple more weeks— cannot drink a beer when he goes to Hooters, as the guys like to do, mostly for the wings and alcohol, partly for the hooters. The other day, in fact, the Hooters girls visited the barracks. People are always visiting Maxwell Hall. Often the wounded warriors are bused off base for field trips—a sailing regatta, a party at a local bar, even a trip to Washington, D.C., to speak to the kids attending the Presidential Classroom. The new guys really seem to enjoy all the fuss. It feels good to be called a hero. The guys who have been here a while enjoy the outings because it's something to do, but they don't like the attention. To a man, they will tell you they ain't no heroes. Heroes are people who fight, not people who get injured.

When you're injured, you can't be a hero—other people become heroes saving your shot-up ass. Although the Hooters girls were wearing their tight little orange shorts when they came to visit the barracks, they didn't bring any wings. Who sends the Hooters girls to visit a bunch of young Marines without any wings? The sense of disappointment in the rec room was palpable.

Leeman's wife is named Brandy. She is twenty-two. Sometimes, at a restaurant, she'll order a beer and give it to him. They live together in a small detached two-bedroom over in married housing; Leeman hangs out at the barracks all day, per orders. Like the other 115 men assigned to Maxwell Hall—some have been here as long as two years—Leeman's job is to attend his doctor's appointments (you pay up to eighty dollars out of pocket if you miss), to take his medicines, to follow doctors' orders... to get well and then to move on, either back to a unit or out of the Corps and into a serviceable rest of his life. Brandy is a friendly and buxom redhead he met at church when he was a junior in high school. It was love at first sight, really. She just thought he was way cute. He is not allowed to say on tape which part of her first attracted him. She gives a hint by placing one hand, palm down, at the level of her shoulders, and the other hand, palm up, at her waist. Brandy used to work the overnight shift at Target, restocking shelves. That's where she was when he called her from the hospital in Al Asad, all doped up on morphine. "Honey, I have a little news." When you're injured, one of the first things they do is give you a phone card with nine hundred free minutes. Leeman doesn't remember whom he called or what he said. Brandy, whose screen name is *JeffreysWoman*, is hoping her husband will soon be well enough to get off LIM DU, limited duty, and start back with PFT, training for the physical-fitness test. She wants him to return to his unit. There is precious little for them to do back home in Lebanon. Not to mention the fact that the Hajis make the *best* blankets. They've gifted them to all their relatives; there are four in the spare bedroom right now. She wants him to send back a few more—and maybe a nice rug for the dining room?

"So me and this friend are watching TV," Ringo continues, "when all of a sudden there's this huge explosion: *Crack!* And I thought, *Damn! Incoming!* Shit, man! I got down and covered up!"

"I fuckin' hate loud noises, man," Romeo concurs.

"No shit," says Cybula.

The high school girl, still holding the toy guitar, turns her head to listen.

"So who was this *friend*, anyways?" Leeman asks, a lascivious tone. His eyes are a little slitty; he's rubbing his nose, too. Though the nightmares have stopped, he still gets bad headaches. His elbow doesn't work the same anymore since the operation. In two days' time, he'll be walking down some steps, and his knee will go out. He's on Percocet, too.

"She's just a friend that I worked with, okay? A *school*teacher. We were watching *television*. Can I just tell my story?"

"I ain't stoppin' ya," Leeman says.

"So I'm down and covered, and my friend screams, like, 'Eek! The house is on fire!' and I'm like, 'What?' and she's like, 'Look! The chimney's on fire!' And I get up from my covered position and I realize—" He stops in his tracks, and his eyes widen, and he thrusts both arms in the air, as if evoking the good Lord in heaven. "A *lightning bolt has just hit the fucking chimney!*"

"No shit!"

"Radical, man!"

"Ya damn skippy," says Ringo, pointing to his fellows like a huckster working the crowd. "See, a lightning bolt came down through the chimney and exploded the gas line in the fake fireplace. And the gas is like woooooooosh—shooting out everywhere, hardcore. And I'm asking her, 'WHERE IS THE FUCKIN' FIRE EXTINGUISHER?' and she's like, 'I DON'T HAVE NO FUCKIN' FIRE EXTINGUISHER!' So I'm like, 'OH, SHIT!' I run outside the house and I find the garden hose, and jump the porch fence and run back inside and already my arm is like fuckin' killing me and I'm like—"

"Hey, Ringo," interrupts Corporal Leeman.

"I'm just getting' to the *good* part, man."

A sober tone from the ranking Marine in the room: "You took a lot of medication, didn't you?"

An impish expression, a sugar-drunk kid: "Why do you ask?"

"'Cause you all hype, tellin' that story. You taking extra?"

"Nah, man, I just didn't have nothin' to eat. I took the shit on an empty stomach."

Leeman stares him down a few long seconds, brother to brother. "Maybe we better go find us some chow," he suggests. "Who's drivin'?"

"Who's payin'?" Cybula asks, leaning way over, pretzeling one hand behind his back, trying in vain to reach an itch.

***

My name is Jeremy Dru Ringgold. I'm twenty-two, from Augusta, Georgia—the great state of Georgia. I spent two tours in Iraq so far. My first tour was 2005-2006. I got injured during my second tour, February 5, 2007.

The way it happened was this: We were at an OP, an observation post, at a water treatment plant on the Euphrates River. The whole area was real pretty—all these pine trees and shit. The first time I was in Iraq, the place I was in was barren desert. But this area was real nice—just a beautiful spot. Whenever we had to go to the water treatment plant, it was like we had the day off. Of course, there was always sporadic small-arms fire, or we'd get a mortar dropped on us, an RPG (rocket-propelled grenade) sent our way. But compared to the rest of the war, being out at this OP was great. It was like having a day off.

So we're sitting there, you know, doing our thing, when the battalion commander comes through. He says that he wants to go up to this spot on the river where we'd been in a firefight previously. It's not a good area. We know it's bad juju up that way. But the colonel's got his own idea. He wants to put a blocking force on the road that's coming from the river. And then he's gonna have a maneuver element sweep up the river and see if they can find any bad guys. For some reason, idiot that I am, I volunteer to go.

I'm part of the blocking force. We move up the road and this boot LT, this green-ass lieutenant, sets us in, puts us in positions. And I'm telling him, "Sir, we really need to find somewhere to put these Humvees in cover, 'cause right here we're exposed." He looks at me and he says, "We're good, lance corporal. If anything happens, we'll be all right." And I'm like, *Yeah right, kiss my ass.* You know what I'm sayin?

Meanwhile, the colonel's detachment starts to maneuver up the river. All of a sudden, this convoy of cars appears on the road, coming our way fast. It's like a stampede coming from the direction we're facing. We set up a snap VCP, which is a real quick vehicle checkpoint. One thing I gotta say: I am terrified of searching cars.

During my first deployment, we had a suicide car bomb take out one of our squads. He killed the point man and took out nine other guys. They were just outside our base. Usually, you know, you go down a street and all these kids are playing—every street you go on, kids are playing. But then you go down another street and it's dead quiet. It's desolate. *Desolate.* And you know something's gonna happen. It's like the movies. One guy says, "It's quiet out here." And the other guy says, "Too quiet." It's one of those situations.

The squad's on patrol on this quiet street when this vehicle pulls out of an alleyway. The driver spots the squad and he puts it into reverse real quick, backs back into the alleyway, which is kind of normal behavior, because if you're a citizen and you see a military patrol, your first instinct is to get the freak out of the way as fast as you can—at least, if you're a friendly and you value your life, which many of these Hajis do not. After the first part of the patrol passed the alleyway, the vehicle pulls out again into the street. The point man, Lance Corporal Anderson, screams, "Everybody get down!" He runs toward the vehicle and opens fire. Then the vehicle detonates. It was a God-awful huge explosion.

When we got there the world was on fire. I seen Marines laying everywhere. It was just one of those things that sticks with ya, those Marines laying everywhere. We had to search for Lance Corporal Anderson. We couldn't find him at first. And then we were like, "What's that big chunk of car layin' over there?" Well, it turns out it wasn't a big chunk of car after all. It was Anderson. He'd been blown to shit and charbroiled. The top of his head was missing, all kinds of nasty shit, whatever. It happens. It's warfare. But that was a rough day. The explosion caught the ground on fire. I remember when we got there, the ground was bubbling. And I was like, *Man, why is the ground bubbling?* Later I found out: When the vehicle detonated, the force of the explosion had broken a water main that was buried underground, so that all the water was bubbling up to the surface. And then there was gasoline floating on top of the water, burning, just floating down to the street in flames. It was one of those surreal things, like *holy shit*, you know what I'm sayin'? It was like some stuff out of a movie, you know, except it was real.

Ever since then, I have not liked searching cars. But here we are. We set up this snap VCP—on this frickin' patrol I volunteered for. And lo and behold, who do you think is assigned to search the frickin' cars?

This is the usual procedure: We stop them about 300 meters from our position. Then we bring them through, one car at a time. We have the male get out, or the driver, which is always a male in Iraq. Then you have him turn around, and you watch him closely, because if somebody's about to blow themselves up, they have this look about them. It's a nervous look—he's about to blow himself to smithereens. You watch them, you see their body language. You gotta figure there's gonna be a certain amount of nervousness to begin with, because they're up against these Americans with guns and shit. But if they're gonna blow themselves up they're usually sweaty and real fidgety. If they're gonna do something, you just know.

The first car pulls up. The guy gets out of the car. He's on the HVT list, high value target. So we PUCed (pronounced *pucked*) him, prisoner under control, meaning that we took him into custody. I strapped flexicuffs on him.

The second car comes through. And *that* guy's on our HVT list, too. And it's like, *Uh-oh*. Alarm bells start going off in my head. We got like nine more cars lined up coming our way, and the first two are HVTs. The third car pulls through. We don't have anything on him, we send him on his way. The fourth car pulls through, nothing on him. By now, I'm starting to feel a little squirrelly. I said to the lieutenant, "Sir, I can't check no more cars today. I'm getting physically sick. I cannot do this." And he said, "Aw, Ringgold, nothing's gonna happen to you." After you check out the driver, you have him open up the car—the doors, the trunk, the hood. You're like, *ifta, ifta, ifta,* all around the car, which is Arabic for "open." After they open everything up, you have them come over to you, *tal, tal, tal,* which is Arabic for "come." You search them good to make sure they're not holding some sort of trigger mechanism, you know, so that while I'm over there looking at the car he can't go *boom* and detonate a bomb. When you're satisfied he doesn't, you go check out the vehicle.

I start searching the engine compartment. Suddenly there's a huge explosion. *BOOM!* It's thunderous. My knees buckle. There's meat flying through the air. Big chunks of meat. I said to myself, *Oh, man, I got a suicide fuckin' bomber.* And then I was like, *How did I miss that?*

Then this guy comes running out of the dust cloud, straight at me. He's one of the Iraqis we just pulled from his car, and he's running out of the dust cloud. And I'm like, *This motherfucker threw a hand grenade!* That was my thought, that maybe he wasn't a car bomber, that maybe he just threw a hand grenade and blew up some Marines. So I kicked him as hard as I could in his knee and took him down to the ground. I put my rifle in the back of his head. I clicked off the safety, set it to "fire."

And right as I started to squeeze the trigger—he was looking up at me, just terrified. I could see it in his eyes, he was saying, "No," you know? He was just wide-eyed. These bright brown eyes. Just the brightest, widest, brownest eyes. And right as I went to squeeze the trigger, I get knocked on my ass.

I'm down on the ground. I said to myself, *Man, what the fuck was that?* I thought it was shrapnel that hit me in the head. 'Cause it just hit me like a ton of bricks, just dropped me, I went right on my ass. It was a stunning blow. I was stunned. I took cover behind the guy that I'd just taken to the ground—I use him like a sandbag, you know, a human sandbag. His ass was toward me. His ass and his back. I get down as low as I can in the dirt behind this guy, and I pull my helmet off, and this is what I see: This here is the helmet

I was wearing. See? The bullet went in the front, here, and came out in the back, there. But it didn't touch my head or nothing. Not a scratch. Have you ever seen the movie *Saving Private Ryan*? There's this scene where this dude gets hit in the helmet and he takes it off to look at it. And his buddy goes, "You're a lucky bastard." And then the guy smiles, you know, and then he gets shot in the head. That's the first thing I thought about. So I said, *Fuck that*. I put my helmet back on my head real quick.

I start putting rounds out across the river, in the direction the fire was coming from. It's the same place it had come from the other day, which is what I was trying to tell the frickin' lieutenant in the first place. My human sandbag was curled up into a fetal position; I had my rifle propped up on his side, on the meat of his hip area, just below the rib cage. I don't know if you've ever felt the overpressure of a barrel. As a round comes out, there's an extreme amount of overpressure; it's enough to make you feel like somebody's hitting you in the head with a hammer. My overpressure on this guy's midsection must've been intense. Meanwhile, I look over to my left and there's our interpreter. He's right near me, curled up in a ball. But he's still got his video camera going. And I remember thinking, *This is gonna be a cool video. I wonder if he got any video of me getting hit in the head?*

In a combat situation, my job is to get my team and to orient their fire—but I didn't have my team out there, remember. I had volunteered for this patrol. I was with a squad I didn't really know. So I start to look around to see what I need to do with this group. As I'm looking around, I see a Marine layin' face down on the ground, about fifty meters away. He's, like, convulsing. His body's twitching back and forth. He's facedown on the ground, and he's not trying to roll back over or anything, which is not a good sign. I said to myself, *Somebody has got to help this Marine, he's in a bad spot.* And then I thought, *This is it. I'm gonna get hit.* I don't know why I thought that. I just did. It just came to me and I said it to myself, calm like that, I just had the feeling. I just knew that by the time I got over there to save that dude... See, when a bullet goes over your head it makes a cracking sound. When you're in a firefight it's like *crack,*

crack, crack, crack everywhere. When a bullet is *real* close to you, it sounds more like a *zip*. This was like *crack, crack, crack, crack* and they were all over the place, a heavy volume of fire. It was not the worst firefight I've ever been in, but we were not in a good position. We were very exposed.

I ran over there as fast as I could, fifty meters, full combat gear, plus all those grenades for my 203, the grenade launcher attached to my M-16. I get to this Marine. He's laying next to this Humvee, near the back-passenger side, facedown. Rounds are hitting the Humvee, like *ping, ping, ping*. I roll him over. He was already dead. I mean, his body—it was a direct hit with an RPG is what had happened. That's how they initiated the firefight. And he was blown to shit. His legs were pretty much blown off. The only reason they were even still there was because of his cammies, the cloth was holding them together.

I get up and I start putting round out to cover my movement, and as I start to move, the battalion gunner comes running up to help this guy. The battalion gunner is a chief warrant officer, the highest rank an enlisted man can attain. You gotta give them the utmost respect. I tell him, "Sir, he's already dead." But I guess he didn't hear me, 'cause he kneeled down anyway. Or maybe he did hear me; maybe he just wanted to see for himself. He probably knew this guy. So instead of me moving away, I stayed there to supply cover, I started putting round out. The gunner is like, no shit, he's kneeling down right in front of me, like almost underneath me, leaning over at dead Marine. And I'm standing above him, putting round out, like *pow, pow, pow, pow*, puttin' rounds out across the river. I wish I had a picture of that, man. I would blow that shit up big and put it on my wall. They could make a statue or some shit outta that scene. Him kneeling over the dead Marine, me standing over them both, putting rounds out, my M16 with its 203 attachment, badass shit.

All of a sudden my arm just, just—I could see it happening in slow motion—it just flew away from me and my weapon fell to the ground. And I was like, *Fuck! I just got hit.* I was more upset than anything. It was like, *Shit, shit, shit!* Like when you're really mad? A frustrated kind of mad. Disappointed. Like *Goddamshit!* I was just pissed to be hit. It didn't really hurt. It felt like somebody was standing on my arm, it just felt like so much pressure. I don't know who I was telling, but I was screaming, "I just got hit!" I was fuckin' screaming it. I picked up my rifle and I tried to use it again. As soon as I squeezed the trigger, that's when the pain really hit me. *Whoa.* It was intense. It was really, really, really—obviously, it was the worst pain I've ever felt, a bullet had just went through my body. It's like nothing I've ever felt before. Just intense pain. It hurt like shit.

I jumped into the front passenger side of the Humvee and yelled to the gunner, "I need a pressure bandage!" He throws me a tourniquet instead. I go, "No, you fucking idiot! I said a *pressure* bandage!" Because a tourniquet is fuckin' gonna cut off the blood and I don't wanna lose my arm. It's not that bad of a wound. And you know I was fuckin' out of my mind because the guy I was yelling at was the battalion gunner, a chief warrant officer. But I guess he realized what was what, because he doesn't say nothin'. He just throws me the pressure bandage. My arm was locked like this, turned down in a fist. My hand won't open, nothing. I can't move it. I can't even get to my own medical pack. That's why I had to get somebody else to hand me something in the first place—you know, we all carry our own first aid supplies. So I go to undo the blousing on my sleeve. It's all covered in blood. I pulled my sleeve down slowly. Some of the muscle was hanging out. And I was like, *Fuck!* But I was also, like, *Okay. I'm not gonna die.* There was this piece of red meat about the size of my pinkie, this dark red meat, and blood was just flowing out of the hole in my arm. It kind of looked like—You know when you drain the oil out of your car? How it just pours out? It's not like drip, drip, drip. It's more like glug, glug, glug. That's what it looked like. Pretty much like the oil draining out of a car.

I wrapped the pressure bandage around my arm. It's pretty much like an Ace bandage except it has a pad on it. You wrap it relatively tight, not tight enough to cut off the circulation, but tight enough. After I'm done, I notice there's this guy standing behind me in the Humvee. He's on the 50-cal, this big machine gun mounted in the turret of the Humvee with armor all around it. But he's all tucked down. He's not shooting. He's obviously boot, never been in combat. Right about this time the gunner looks into the Humvee and yells at the guy, "You better start fuckin' shooting!" But the boot guy leans down and goes, "I don't know what to shoot at!" I grab him by his pant leg, and I yelled to him, "Look up at the fuckin' windows across the river and light them bitches up!" And he's like, "Roger *that*," and he starts firing his 50-cal, *jub, jub, jub, jub, jub,* just rockin' the Humvee. At that point I forgot all about my pain. I was feeling super motivated, you know, like *Fucking-a-right!* I wanted to blow somethin' up, you know what I'm sayin'? Fuck this injury shit. My boys were out there dyin'. So I go to get out of the Humvee and the gunner just like reaches over and throws me back in. And he's like, "You're not getting out of the fucking Humvee." And I was like, "Roger that, sir." So at that point it was game over for me.

Then it came time for evac. They put all the pieces of the Marine who had been blown up—the guy I got hit trying to save—on the front hood of my Humvee. And they drove me and him down to the farmlands to where they were gonna land the bird to medivac us out. Like I said, I wasn't out with my squad that day. I was just subbing in with another squad for that patrol. And as I get out of the Humvee to go get on this bird—I'm walking, you know, I'm ambulatory—I see that my regular squad is there. It's *my* guys securing the area for the bird to land.

When they seen who it was wounded, two of my best buds came running up. They was about to grab my arm to help me with it, but I said, "Don't touch, it fuckin' hurts." One was a guy named Orris, and the other one's a guy named Lance Corporal Dmitruk. On my first tour, Dmitruk's arm got blown in half. His bone was blown out. But they patched him up and now he was back in Iraq on his second tour with me. When Dmitruk was wounded, it was me and Orris who helped *him*. We put pressure on his arm, so he didn't bleed out, we wrapped his arm up in a tourniquet, we put him on the bird. So it's kind of funny that Orris and Dmitruk met me and put me on the bird. That was the last time I got to see them—those guys, my squad, any of them. One thing that kind of gets lost is the real, like, the kind of brotherly bond that Marines have. I can look at one of my Marines and be like, *I love that guy.* I'll tell him, too. I'll tell him, "Hey man, I love ya." I learned that from my first tour. Because you can be sitting there one second with a buddy of yours and then the next second that bad boy's on a bird, all burned to shit, all blown to shit, what have you. So I have no problem telling my guys, "Hey dude: I love you." 'Cause you never know, he could go out on patrol, step on a bomb, and be done.

Then, I'm sittin' on the bird and we're being flown out of there. It's a CH-46 Sea Knight. I don't know if you've ever been on a 46. It's got the twin rotors. With both the rotors going, it actually shakes the whole helicopter like a damn washing machine. So I'm sittin' on the bird, shaking. And the Marine who'd been killed was in there too. That was the first time I'd ever seen him. I'd never met the guy. He had real curly brown hair, and I was lookin' at him. And the corpsman was like, "Are you okay?" He kept getting in my face. "Are you okay? Are you okay?" And I said, "I'm good. I'm gonna live. I'm going home."

When we landed, they tried to take me off the bird first. And was like, "Nah, he's gettin' off first," meaning the dead Marine. And they're like, "No, you're getting off first." And I said, "You're gonna take him off first or I'm just going to sit in here and we're gonna have problems." So they took him off the bird and then I got off the bird.

When I got back to the States, I was at Andrews Air force base. I had literally just landed, and I got a phone call from a staff sergeant back here at Camp Lejeune. And he's like, "Lance Corporal Van Perry's parents would like to speak to you." And I was like, "Who is that?" And he's like "That's the Marine that got killed when you got hit." He gave me their number, but it took me a little while for me to call them. I just had to prepare myself first, 'cause I didn't know what they were going to want to talk about, though I knew they were going to obviously want to know what happened. Finally, I just called. It wasn't too bad. They asked how I was feeling and everything. They were obviously upset. They wanted to know how their son had died. So I told them. I said, you know, that he was hit with the first round, the opening salvo, so to speak. It was an RPG, a rocket-propelled grenade. So it was a direct hit with an RPG. He was dead as soon as it hit him. I found out when the funeral was and I went up there to Arlington National Cemetery, in Virginia. I was obviously really, really sedated, because I'd only been hit ten days prior. My arm was jacked. I didn't wear a uniform. I just wore some civilian clothes. My wife took me up there. I never actually met the family before. They probably were like, "Who is this guy with his arm all taped to hisself?"

At Arlington there was four funerals going on at the same time. You could hear all of them going on at once. There was the funeral I was at, a funeral over here, a funeral up on the hill, and another funeral in the valley. All for guys who'd been killed in Iraq. It was about 3:00 in the afternoon. The sun was out. The snow was pretty thick. It was an awesome sight—the military honor guards, the Marines in their dress blues, all those white crosses gleaming in the sun. It was beautiful.

People die in warfare. Warfare will always be. No matter what people think—world peace, whatever—warfare will always happen. If you take away all the guns in the world, I'm coming at you with a club. One thing I never realized until I went to war was that the guys who die in wars are so young. I mean, you just don't think about or realize how young they are. I was nineteen when I went on my first tour. I could have died at nineteen. There's so much more about life that I've learned from nineteen to twenty-two. These guys get mowed down in their prime. They never get to learn that shit. The vast majority of people killed in action, in any war, are young guys. So when I looked at those crosses lined up, I just thought, you know, of all those young lives.

***

Another morning, Corporal Kinnee is in the rec room. His tunic is half on and half off. He can't seem to get his left arm to go through the rolled-up sleeve. The roll is tight. The arm is rubbery. Think of a time when you woke up in the middle of the night and your arm was totally asleep, just dead meat. That's Kinnee's arm pretty much, except for the little bit he can squeeze his hand—the grip not as strong as a newborn baby's. His shoes are untied, his trouser bottoms are unsecured. He has asked one of the sergeants to help him finish dressing.

"When it gets past my elbow, I'm good," Kinnee explains.

"We'll git ya," the gunnery sergeant says reassuringly, meanwhile struggling a bit, trying to force the inanimate hand through the tight roll of cloth. Sometimes, Gunny's vision will all of a sudden flick off, like a shorted-out light bulb. It can last a minute or a day. So far, it has always returned.

They are standing in the far corner of the room, near the vibrating recliners. Devil Dogs watch the big screen, play pool, doze in chairs. There is a general morning heaviness in the air, the groggy feel of a hangover. Gunny is making scant progress. His lips are pursed and grim.

"Just cut it off," Kinnee says. "It might be easier. Shit. It don't even work."

"You might want it someday. Isn't there some indication it'll get better?"

"Yeah, there is. I'm just joking around. I don't want my arm cut off. I like it. I've had it for twenty-six years. I can't really see using some metal claw."

"How about we just loosen this sleeve a bit, take off one of the rolls."

"But it was lookin' *good*," Kinnee protests.

"It needs to be a little looser, pardner," Gunny says gently. He begins unrolling.

"Aw, *mannnnnn*," groans Kinnee.

"Don't worry. I won't make it look bad."

"Corporal Love usually does it for me. He makes 'em *tight*."

"You don't need 'em tight right now," says the gunny, a little annoyed. "Unless somebody's gonna be there to help you take them off, you'll be in trouble."

I'm not *takin'* 'em off," Kinnee says, a tad petulant.

***

My name is John Cybula. I'm twenty-one, from Sweetwater, Tennessee. About the only thing famous there is this underground cave that has a waterfall and stuff. It's about two hours from Nashville—depends on how you drive. I lived there with my grandparents most of my life. I never knew my dad 'till I was seventeen. My grandpa is retired from the Marine Corps. He owns three Sonics—the fast food restaurants. He used to work me some crazy hours. He's one of those guys, like, when you work for him—I remember this one time I got in a car accident and he still made me go to work. I used to get up at 3:00 in the morning to go do the early prep and stuff like that. I'd be doing hours that weren't even counted on the clock, but I mean, it's a family thing, you know? He always took care of me, so it's the least I owed him. He was the one that pushed me in the direction of the Marine Corps. It surprised the heck out of my family when I joined, because I was the guy that wasn't supposed to do anything with my life. I wasn't really a mess-up in high school, I was just one of the dumb jocks. Like, I was the guy that didn't do my work, but I passed because I was the quarterback. I played for Mid-County High School. I was pretty good. I wasn't no college material, I'll tell you, but I was good for the high school level, I guess you'd say. You know the scene: the cheerleaders, the babes, the crowd, stuff like that. It's kinda funny now that I think about it. Seems like a long time ago.

When I was a freshman in high school, I weighed eighty-six pounds. I had the bowl cut going on—my mom used to cut my hair herself. She really used a bowl. When I was younger, I had this crew cut. I used to get the Batman logo cut into the back of my head. I thought that was the stuff, back in the day. Or then, another time, I had the Nike swoosh. It was like the trademark thing to do. It was trendy. Eventually, my mom and I lived separate. We had some family issues and stuff like that. Not child abuse, but my step dad and me used to get into it pretty bad. I was a real mess back then, totally white like a ghost—I looked anorexic. Then I moved in with my grandparents for good. I went up to 150 my sophomore year, and then by my senior year I bumped up to five foot eleven, 200. So I was getting healthy and stuff like that. It was cool. When I came back to high school that fall, the girls were like, "Wow, who are you?" And I was like, "Hey, it's me, John." And they were like, "Oh, my God!"

My first tour I went to Afghanistan. That was a pushover. We didn't do much. My second tour I went to Iraq. When we first got there, it was calm; it was relatively nice. I don't mean *nice*, but all you'd hear usually was sporadic fire—nothing towards us. Then it got bad. They turned the war up a few notches, I guess you can say. I remember the first time I shot somebody. That's probably my favorite combat story.

I remember it was night. We were doing house checks to search for weapons and stuff like that. We got to this one house. It was right behind the big blue mosque in Fallujah. Me and my squad, we go up on this roof, and there's chickens all over, so we start kicking 'em off the roof and laughing about it, just laughing and kicking these chickens off the roof. I don't know why we was doing it. Just something to pass the time, something for laughs, you know. That's how guys are.

Then we go back downstairs. We're in the courtyard. Every house is built like that, with a courtyard and a front gate. We noticed a group of men outside the gate, in the street, all congregated together. And what happened was, I had this squad leader named Sergeant Beach. He went out the front gate, and I followed. He noticed that one of them had a grenade in his hands and was going to throw it. After giving the proper warning, he shot one round. I shot three rounds and killed the dude—double tapped him in the chest and hit him once in the artery in the leg. He was dead instantly, I think. And I remember when I first did it, right after I shot the guy, right after I saw him land on the ground. I don't know why, but I turned around to the SAW gunner, his name was Lance Corporal Pugh, and I said, "I just killed that guy." And Pugh was like, "Yes, you did." And we was all laughing about it, you know, because I must of had this expression on my face, this look like, *Wow, look what I just did.* 'Cause it didn't really hit me. It was all, like, muscle memory. It was automatic. You see somebody posing a threat to you, you're gonna raise your weapon and shoot. You don't think about it. That's what they train us to do. So that's basically what happened. And that's my all-time favorite combat story. It's not action-packed or nothing like that, but most of my other combat stories deal with losing somebody. In this one, nobody I know gets hurt. Maybe that's why it's my favorite.

I lost two good friends over there. One was Corporal Snyder. He got shot in the back of the head by a sniper on post. And it just so happened I was his medivac. I was in the Humvee with him, holding his head on the way to Fallujah Surgical. He died in my arms right there. That hurt me real bad. And then we had a Corporal Albert Gettings. He was like the best squad leader I ever had. The way he got hit, the way he conducted himself—it was just heroic. He got shot by this sniper and fell to the ground. But then he got right back up and started returning fire—even though he had this bad stomach wound. Then another guy behind him got hit; he dragged that guy to safety and was *still* returning fire. Finally, we got him to lay down. By then he'd lost too much blood. They couldn't get enough blood back into him in time, so he passed away. That was the worst ever, right there.

As far as myself, I'm okay. I'm in a lot of pain right now, like my hip really hurts bad—when I fell off that roof, I broke my pelvis in three pieces. It's been about eighteen months now since my injury. I'm on a lot of meds. I just have to deal with it. People don't realize: Yeah, we get hurt and stuff like that, but you don't always go back to perfect. That's my case right now. I'd like to go back to my unit. I'd like to get back to Iraq. What they're probably gonna do is put me on a PEB, which is a physical evaluation board. They will say if I'm well enough to go back to my duties. Seeing how my hip's pretty bad busted, they're gonna probably end up pushing me out.

At first, the initial thought after the injury was, "Hey, this guy's hip is gonna heal back together, he's gonna be fine, he's going to return back to full duty." And that's what I did at first. I healed up, I rejoined my unit. But then, about the second day back, I hurt it again. I had this bad limp for like six months. That's the whole mentality of a grunt, you know. *Suck it up, it'll be okay, you'll get over it.* And I dealt with it for a long time. But it started getting worser and worser and worser. Finally, it was to the point where I couldn't even ride in a car and hit a bump, that's how bad it got. And I mean, don't get me wrong, the first surgery I had after that, it helped me a little bit. They did a hip scope basically, and scraped off all the bad cartilage. And, like, my bone had overgrown when it repaired itself, so it was popping out of the socket. They had to shave off some of that stuff, trying to get it to quit doing that. They told me I'd probably have complications, but at least I can walk now without a bad limp. That's the only good part. I used to limp bad. Like it used to be so bad I couldn't even walk down stairs.

Right now, I'm waiting to see if I can get another surgery to make me better. But they're kind of like, "No, you just need to get out of the Marine Corps." I'll tell you one thing: I'm not gonna do no desk job. I didn't join the Marine Corps to do no desk job. I don't sign papers; I make papers get signed. That's just how I feel about things, I'd rather by shooting at shit. It's just my mentality. I'm 03-11 Infantry. A rifleman. I didn't pass the knowledge test, or I'd be a machine gunner. To be honest with you, rifleman was my main choice anyway, because basically, I wanna be right there, kickin' doors in, stuff like that. I'm not saying it fascinates me; it's just what I like to do. I love the whole mentality—I love to be in firefights, I love the adrenaline rush, I love everything about it. I mean, it has its bads, you know. You lose friends, you lose a lot of people and stuff like that. It blows big-time. But you just gotta suck it up and deal with what you got. Freedom isn't free. You know what I mean?

Right now, I'm not regretting anything. Like, I'm not regretting anything that I did. I don't regret going. I don't regret getting shot and falling through that hole in the roof. I don't regret not getting my Purple Heart. I don't regret killing nobody. Not really. I did what I did because I feel like this: I'm keeping *them* over *there*. I'm keeping them from coming back over here and doing another 9/11. There's a lot of people who got lost in 9/11. That's one of the big reasons I joined. I remember sitting in the classroom and seeing that on TV, and I was like, "Yeah! I'm joining the military!" I was a sophomore in high school. I was sitting in the science classroom. And I remember they turned the TVs on, and like at first, everybody thought, *This is something from Hollywood. Somebody is messing with us. This is some kind of bull crap.* But then it set in that it really happened. And you kind of felt, like, *Wow, we just got hit on our home shores. Somebody brought the fight to us.* I wish I coulda joined up that minute. I woulda went right then if I could have, but I was too young. So that's how it is. That's my motivation. Honestly, I'm not doing this for the money—ha ha, right? The main reasons I went into the Marine Corps was because I was so pissed off at what happened on 9/11. I'm not sayin' I went over there for revenge. I just went over there to keep them over there.

When I first got back, there were a lot of bad things happening to me. Like, that's what happened with my marriage. My wife— my soon-to-be-ex-wife—she was a psych tech, a Navy chick from Albany, New York. We fell in love very fast. I mean, once you know you love somebody, you know. We just knew it. We had our fallouts, we had our fights and stuff like that, but something always brought us back together. Finally, we were like, "Hey, let's get married," so we got married. I'm glad I tied the knot. I love her to death—or at least I did, until she cleaned out my bank account, the bitch, pardon my French. I don't know why she had to go and do that for. It's funny sometimes what people do. Not funny, *ha ha*, you know. Funny *strange*. Fucked up, you know? But I have to give her one thing: She helped me get through some stuff. There were times when I first got back that I didn't know what I'd do without her. She took care of me and everything, 'cause, like, I had a lot of bad things going on—the nightmares, the recurrences, stuff like that. For the first six months I was back, I dream about falling off that building. I dreamed constantly about that. Or not every night. It would alternate between falling off a building and seeing Corporal Gettings get shot. And then seeing the kids that we shot—that we had to shoot because they had grenades. Every time I went to sleep, I'd see all the recurrences of all the bad times, you know, stuff that made an impact on your mind.

Basically, what happens is you're sleeping, and you're re-enact what happened. Those are your dreams. It seems pretty real. You wake up either in a cold sweat, or sometimes I'd wake up swinging.

It just depends. Thank God I never did that to my wife. I think the reason I didn't was because when she was around, I had that closeness. Like in the Marine Corps, when you go to sleep at an OP or something, all your buddies are all around you, making sure you're safe, and you feel better. But when you're alone, you're just like... You feel like you're in a corner, you know? So I think about my wife, when she was with me and stuff, well, I just slept better knowing there was someone there with me. I feel safer, basically.

You try to forget about things, and you try to put them out of your mind, but the dreams just bring them back. It opens that wound back up, makes you scared. It just depends on what you dream about. If I see Corporal Gettings, I get really sad. I have trouble sleeping at night, because I don't wanna dream about that crap. I really don't wanna go through it again. I'm going to appointments and stuff for it now, so it should be getting better. I got to talk therapy; they help you out with meds, too, like they give you stuff to make you go to sleep. One major drug they put you on is this stuff that blocks you from dreaming. It keeps you from going into REM sleep or something. You don't dream. Either that you don't remember what you dream, I forget which.

The worst thing about all of this is leaving the guys. Ever since I got whacked, the only thing that really hurt me the whole time was like—I really wanted to be back with my guys. When you're with your unit, you're like a family. You're a big family. That's your brothers around you. And leaving your family always sucks. You don't wanna leave your brothers. It's like, they have your back, and you have theirs. You're willing to give up your life for the guy on your left and the guy on your right, and they're willing to give up their lives for you. So it's like trying to take a little kid from his mom. It ain't gonna happen. You're going to scream and kick and do all you can do to stay back. That's just basically how it is.

***

Master Sergeant Ken Barnes is the second in command of Maxwell Hall—at least for the time being, until they get a replacement for

Lieutenant Colonel Maxwell. Born in Montana, raised all over, he joined the Marines at seventeen. Now, he's got twenty years in. He served with Maxwell in Iraq in the 24th MEU (pronounced *mew*, Marines Expeditionary Unit), a fighting force of about 1,200, deployed to trouble spots around the world via Navy fleet, the historic mission of Marines dating back to ancient Greece. From the day Maxwell briefed him on his idea for a Wounded Warrior Barracks, Barnes worked hard to help get the concept off the ground. Sometimes, he muses, it felt like they were running a three-legged race—two guys all shot to shit, diminished, they pooled their resources, made things happen despite the odds.

Hard and sardonic, at once a cynic and a true believer, Barnes is your textbook senior noncom, noncommissioned officer. He's exchanged live fire in Liberia, in Somalia, in George Bush senior's Desert Storm, in George junior's post-Saddam Iraq. As it happened, Barnes joined the 24th only six days before it left for Iraq. He was a gunnery sergeant at the time, assigned to lead the personal security detachment of the MEU commander, Colonel Ronald Johnson (since promoted to brigadier general). As a kid, Barnes had dreamed of becoming an Air Force pilot. After he started wearing glasses at age eleven, he settled on wanting to be an Air Force MP, military policeman. When he discovered you had to be twenty-one to carry a gun in the Air Force, he opted for the Marines, following in the footsteps of this stepfather, who had gone on to make a small fortune in concrete. "I was a good grunt all the way through," Barnes says, "but what I really like was working security detachments. It's that MP thing come back to haunt me, I guess. The best way to describe it is like the secret service guarding the president. The colonel was our president. You're on the road all the time, you're moving all the time, you're in the middle of shit all the time. It's like leading your own platoon. The only officer that is really in charge of you is the guy you're protecting. When this billet came open, I was teaching machine gunnery at the School of Infantry. You better believe I jumped at the chance."

As Colonel Johnson's security man, Barnes worked closely with Johnson's OpsO, his operations officer, Lieutenant Colonel Maxwell.

"First thing I could tell about Maxwell was that he was smart as hell," Barnes remembers. "You could tell that operationally, he had his finger on that entire MEU—all 1,200 men. There was no bullshit about him. And when you get a guy like that, you know, whether he's chewing your ass or he's giving an order or just sitting around and shootin' the shit, that's what it is. It's no bullshit. He's not gonna hide anything from you. He's gonna give it to you straight whether you like it or not; he's not gonna dance around the issues. He was firm but fair. On some occasions, when I was pissed off or whatever, I could go in his office and shut the door and rant and rave. Maxwell would sit back, and he'd be like, "Alright, Guns (he was a gunnery sergeant at the time), get you a cup of coffee—go ahead and vent, buddy." I'd get it off my chest and I'd be good.

"See, any time Colonel Johnson left that FOB for anything, whether it was to go up to Baghdad or to Ramadi, or to visit somebody, or to check on something—anytime he moved one inch off the base, I had to arrange all the travel and security. Colonel Johnson was not one to shy away from a fight. If shit was blowing up and people were shooting, he felt like he needed to be there. Working for him, you knew that going in. You couldn't be a candy ass, because we were there to keep him alive. He relied on us every second of the day to make sure that if he did get into a shit sandwich that we got him out. So it was just a great job. I had a great relationship with the colonel. He's like one of those big uncle-kind of guys that you could really get along with—though occasionally he'd piss me the fuck off, which is when I'd go into Max's office and rant and rave.

"The day was November 2, 2004. For some reason, we were escorting a British convoy of minesweepers. I never understood that mission, because they had more armor than we did. The minesweepers themselves were escorted by M113s, which are armored personnel carriers, so they have more armor than my Humvees do—they're just a tad bit slower. But it was a push from division. That was what they wanted us to do. The colonel even tried to wave it off, but then the next thing I knew he was calling me back into his office and telling me, 'We're doing this mission.' And I was like, 'Roger that, sir,' 'cause that's my job, to do what the colonel tells me even if I thought it was crazy.

"I was riding in the turret of the Humvee. That was usual for me. We didn't have the full shield back then, it was just the front gunner shield. To me, riding in that position was just the easiest way to control a lot of stuff. If we were running in a convoy, I had to be able to see everything. I certainly couldn't see from *inside* the Humvee. I always rode in the command vehicle. I had the colonel in one seat, I had a shooter in another seat, and I had my driver. And then, I needed a seat for the sergeant major, because he liked to ride with the colonel too. I had to be able to see all the vehicles behind me, and I had to be able to see all the vehicles in front of me. When you run a hundred meters of dispersion on fast roads, when you're runnin' sixty-five, seventy miles an hour, with one hundred meters between each of the five vehicles, well, that's a long way if the front vehicle gets hit. That's a long way if the back vehicle gets hit. Somebody's got to be able to see all that stuff to control it. Having been a machine gunner before, I know how to use the machine gun better than anybody in my section; I *instructed* it for three years. Who better to have on the gun on the move? Now, when the colonel got *out* of the vehicle, we had to have somebody from the dismount truck come back and man that machine gun for me, because I would always accompany the colonel, which kind of made it a little bit awkward, but it doesn't really matter—that's just how we ran it. The colonel was totally cool with it. He was like, 'Do it how you think you ought to, Guns.'

"When you're on patrol, when you're driving places, when you're on foot patrol, when you're going anywhere, you have to constantly be aware of everything. Every person, every car, every piece of trash. In Iraq, the ground is covered with trash. Literally. Everywhere you go, there is a carpet of trash. A landscaping of trash. There's all kinds of shit. There's dead animals. There's dead people. And they put IEDs in everything. They don't give a shit, they will put them in a dead body, anything. So you gotta keep super aware when you're over there. Anytime you go anywhere, your eyes are peeled. But you can't see everything. You can only suspect everything. It hardly matters. Sooner or later, it's your turn."

Without warning, a 1,000-pound IED, planted by the side of the road, was detonated. Barnes remembers a bright flash, intense pain, his hand going numb. He thought he'd lost the hand. He looked down at the end of his arm where it used to be and there was just a big hole that was bleeding everywhere. The tendons of the first two fingers were severed, the thumb tendon was severed, the artery was severed. The wrist was shattered into little itty-bitty pieces. The shrapnel went clean through the wrist bone. The doctor told him that if it hadn't been for the way he wore his watch, facedown, the hand would have been completely detached.

Now he's behind this desk, in an office near the rec room of Maxwell Hall, his feet up like an executive, fiddling in midair with a golf club the way men do. A bunch of the more senior Wounded Warriors are being treated to golf this coming weekend at a resort in Myrtle Beach. His grip is totally fucked. He played anyway. As physical injuries go, his is permanent and annoying. The top half of the hand—his thumb and first two fingers—has no feeling at all. The bottom two fingers and the base tingle all the time, pins and needles. The hand is constantly in pain. It is constantly an inconvenience—try pulling down your fly without using your thumb—but it is not life-threatening, he's quick to point out. Sometimes he pays no attention; sometimes it bugs him. On some days it's really bad. At one point, he talked to his doctors about amputation because he was seeing guys do more with prosthetics than he could do with what remained of his real hand. He was on meds for nine or ten months. Pain meds. Sleep meds. Anxiety meds. There was a nerve drug to calm the pain. "The problem was, it didn't just target one nerve in the body, it targeted every single one. I felt like I was trying to walk through mud." Finally, he said to himself, *I'm not takin' this shit no more.*

"I'm glad I got off the pain meds," he says, worrying his grip, searching evermore for a solution, for the ultimate one-and-a-half-handed grip. The acoustic tile ceiling above his head has been partially removed. There is a leak in the roof, white shit all over the shelves and the floor. The contractor has promised to get to it. "Do I hurt? Yep. Does it bug me? Yeah. Do I still have bad dreams? Yeah. Do I still have anxiety attacks? Yeah. I get all that stuff. But to me, it's better to feel like shit than to feel like I'm drowning or like I'm trying to get through a puddle of mud. If I don't sleep, I don't sleep. That's it. I'll get up, play on the computer, watch some TV, stand out in the yard at 2:00 in the morning and swing a golf club. It just doesn't matter. If I can't sleep, I can't sleep. If my hand hurts, my hand hurts. You rub it, you pay attention to it, you don't bump it—eventually, it settles itself down. As far as bad dreams, I've had bad dreams since I was, you know—everybody has nightmares. When you were a kid, you had nightmares. So, to me, it's the same thing. You wake up startled and sweating and holy shit, what was that, and then you take a deep breath, you go get a glass of water, you look under the bed like Mom told you—there's no bogeyman. Then, you either go to sleep or you don't.

"To me, the worst dreams are the ones when you're awake," he continues. "It's almost like an anxiety attack. Something triggers it, and you start to drift off mentally and kinda disconnect from where you're at, which is a little dangerous, especially when you're driving. That's when a lot of 'em tend to happen to me. It's different for everybody. In time, you start to recognize what's happening. I still have a hard time driving past a parked vehicle. You know, you're driving down the road here in the United States, it's not uncommon to see a vehicle parked on the side of the road. Maybe somebody's car broke down, maybe it's out of gas, what have you. If I'm driving on a two-lane road, seeing a car like that will send me almost over the edge. Still today. It really—I still grip the steering wheel. I consider the possibility—what if? What if that car is loaded with explosives? What if it's going to blow up any second? You start going through that and then it triggers *other* things, and before you know it, you're off and running. Then you really have to get a grip on yourself, you just have to pull off to the side of the road. You're like, *All right, asshole. Settle down. You're okay. Ain't nothin' but a car beside the road, some piece of shit that broke down.*

"It's like this TBI business. At first, I just thought I was just tired. I thought maybe it was the pain medication. But when I came off the medication, I realized. It's still really hard to remember stuff that's happening fast. It's like, if stuff is going on, you know, if things at work are going *boom, boom, boom, boom,* you have to deal with the things that come up one at a time, in rapid succession. And I'll do that. But then I'll be doing something else, and all of a sudden, I will think, like, 'What in the hell did I just do?' Or somebody will come in the next day and say, 'You ordered me to do such and such.' And I'll be like, 'Why would I tell you to do that?'

"Focus is another thing. It's very hard. I used to be able to focus on four or five different things at once and keep everything on track. I used to be able to have two or three different missions running, you know, things happening around you all of the time, *bang, bang, bang, bang, bang.* Now, now it's really hard to focus on anything. I used to love to read books. I grew up reading books. That's what you did in your spare time when you're on the float, long months at sea on Navy transports. I'd read four, five, six novels while I was overseas. But I can't read books anymore because I don't have the focus to keep track. You read a chapter, you know, and by the time you hit the second chapter, you're like, 'What the fuck happened in the first chapter?' What's funny," he says, raising his hands to indicate the bookshelves in his office, and those as well that line the rec room, "is we have so many books around here. Look at all those bookshelves. My kids and my wife are all like, 'God, you don't read anymore.' And they're right. I *don't* read anymore. I tell 'em I don't have time to read. I used to love it. Just can't do it anymore. You move on, you know? Even stuff like hunting is affected. Like, I used to absolutely love to hunt. Now it's very hard for me to get the patience level to stay out in a tree stand now and wait for a deer. I just can't focus for that long.

"Sometimes you get frustrated, of course. You ask yourself: *What the fuck?* You know what I mean? You ask yourself, *Why did I get blown up?* What I try to do is look at it in the way that, well if I *hadn't* had got blown up, then Maxwell wouldn't have had somebody he knew that he could go to, somebody who was strong enough at the time to help get all of this started. And I damn sure know he'd never have found anybody to run it for the first year like we ran it. So, you know, it's just one of those things that I say if I had *not* gotten hurt, we woulda never started this barracks. Or maybe somebody would have started it, but it wouldn't be what it is. It's a huge fuckin' deal to me to watch this happen. Because when we first got hurt, this kind of barracks wasn't available. You look all the way back to Vietnam, to Korea, to World War II. Those guys spent all this time in the hospital, but then they were discharged, there was nobody to look after 'em. Nobody who could really understand. It's like, back during the Civil War—"

"Excuse me... Master Sergeant? You sent for me?"

A young grunt, call him Lance Corporal Mario, is knocking on the frame of the open door. A good-looking kid, a little on the short side. Plucky, you can tell, like the Italian-from-Queens guy in one of the old black-and-white movies about soldiers in World War II. His mouth is a little crooked, making it appear as if he is talking out of the side of his face like Popeye.

Barnes points his golf club accusingly: "You got a drug problem, Marine?"

Taken aback: "What?"

"Do... you... have... a... drug... problem?"

Indignant: "I *wish*."

"Why aren't you taking them?" Barnes asks.

"I took 'em," Mario protests. "You can prove it with the blood test."

"That's the problem. The blood test is saying that you *don't* have the drugs in your system."

"I do. I *do*. They just keep telling me to put more and more poison inside myself."

"Well," says Barnes, practicing his golf stroke again from his seated position, "they're obviously not gonna tell you to take something that's gonna kill you."

"I took ten milligrams."

"Well, that's not enough. You have to take what they tell you. They want you on that much because you have a potential for blood clots."

"They're just feeding me rat poison."

"Look, I take the same shit they use to make nuclear weapons, and I still stick it in my mouth every day."

In walks Sergeant D, a six-six string bean with a tattoo for every year he's been in the Corps. He gapes at Barnes with mock horror. "You stick what in your mouth every day? Maybe you gentlemen need to be left alone."

***

My name is Corporal Bobby Joseph. I got no middle name. I've done five deployments in all: Iraq three times, Afghanistan once. The other time I was on a MEU. Tomorrow's my birthday. I'll be twenty-five.

I was born in Smithfield, North Carolina, but I was raised in Naples, Florida. You can call me Bobby or you can call me Joseph or you can call me Jo-Jo, everyone does. Or you can call me Ruthless—I got that name after my deployment in 2003. That Jason mask hanging from the rearview mirror of my Chevy Avalanche? That's Jason from the horror movies. I got that mask to sort of commemorate the name, 'cause I'm a killer. In 2005, I got the name Darkness. As you can see, I'm pretty dark. That was always the big joke in my family, how I was so dark and how my parents were so white—my adoptive parents. At nighttime, it's hard to find me. I creep up on people. I take their weapons. I'm all up in their shit. But I also got a lighter side. That's the side I have when I'm back in the States. Most people only see that—my sunny disposition. I'm known for keeping up the morale. I'm gonna get a tattoo soon. It's gonna say "333" because I'm only *half* evil.

Right now, I'm just laying up in my room. Yesterday, I got my Purple Heart. They had this guy who came to give it to me. He won the Congressional Medal of Honor. He told his whole story. There was this battle in Vietnam, and it was his first patrol, and they were being attacked on three sides; this was back in the day, 1965, I think he said. Then he pinned on my Purple Heart. The day before that, I got my NAM, my Navy and Marine Corps Achievement Medal. That's it over there on my desk. The narrative part talks about how I lead this assault on an enemy position. You can read it for yourself. It's all in there. It's been a big week for me, I guess.

Right now, I'm just lyin' up in the room, on the couch. My leg is sore. I took some pain meds. I got Cartoon Network on the big TV. Got my boy Al Pacino on the wall over there. You ain't gangsta if you don't have your *Scarface* memorabilia. And hanging up there on the other wall is my Dress Blues. When you have that stack on there, the ribbon rack over the pocket, they call it the Dress Blue Bravos. If you put your medals on there, they would be Dress Blue Alfas. That reminds me, I gotta get over to the PX and get me another ribbon rack. It's easier to get around now that I'm off crutches. You should have seen me when I was in the wheelchair. I was a stone demon in that chair. We had these fancy electric ones that got donated. Fingertip control. At least now I'm down to the cane and this walking boot. It stabilizes the ankle and the foot. I asked them to put me upstairs so I would have to climb up and down. It's a bitch, but ain't nobody gonna help me get better but me. I can use the extra PT, physical therapy.

There's nothin' like being in pain for a long time. My shrink is like, "Are you frustrated? Are you getting mad? Are you feeling short-tempered?" And I'm like, "NO! I'm *not* fuckin' mad! What do you fuckin' think?" Everybody has to go to the shrink. Mandatory. I don't go anymore. I told 'em I'm not crazy. I told 'em, "Every time you schedule me an appointment to come to you guys, the more pissed I get. Because I'm not crazy. There's no point in me coming to you. I'm not gonna kill myself or whatever." But yes, I am pissed off that I got blown up. And I'm pissed off that I can't play basketball or run around with my sons or you know, something like that, the normal things, the simple things. I'm stayin' in here rotting away, just waiting for some procedures and appointments that I have to do just to get out the military. It's gonna be a while. I have to have patience. And I do, for the most part. It's just that at some points, you know, you get sick of it. I try to maintain the attitude. I try to keep myself busy. It's like the tattoo idea. When you bored you come up with the weirdest things. I mean, all we have is time. Fuckin' time. You know what I mean?

I joined on September 17, 2001. The recruiters had been trying to get me in high school, but I kept dodging away. I was like, "No,

I'm not joining the military, you guys are crazy." I was like, "I'm gonna go to college and move on." I was probably going to get a business management degree and open a business. I didn't know exactly what I wanted to do. I had two choices. One, go to college. Or two, work for my dad doing landscaping, because I was really good at it, and it's really good money down in Florida. He does landscape maintenance. He does the whole thing: sprinkler systems, once a week service, edging, mowing, fertilizing, mulching, planting sod. I mean, you won't believe the houses he does on Marco Island—half-million-dollar houses. He does 'em for maybe $1,700 a month. Good money.

My parents have been taking care of me for a while. I'm adopted. It was a little weird, growing up. I would see my skin color, and then I'd look at theirs, and I was like, "What's wrong with me?" In Naples, where I grew up, they had a ghetto. It's called Golden Gate. Everybody calls it Ghetto Gate. There's black people in there. But where I grew up, it was downtown. There were nothing but rich white people. I was the only black person there. Everybody knew me. Then we moved to Golden Gate because the traffic in downtown Naples was horrible. My parents bought a house—four bedrooms, three baths, two living rooms, a swimming pool, all that. You could live pretty good there if you had some money. When I was about seven or eight years old, I met my real parents. Now they live in Golden Gate too. So me going home is a pain in the butt, because both of them wanna see me. Everybody wants me to come over and eat. Before, I had no parents. Now, I got too many parents. Life is weird like that. It's like a pain in the butt. So I just stay at my girlfriend's house—there I have no drama. All in all, I had a pretty good upbringing. They called me a spoiled brat.

Then, 9/11 happened. I was pissed off. I had friends and family up there in New York. And I was like, "You know what? Let's see what I can do to help." So I went and talked to a recruiter. And he was like, "What do you want to do?" And I said, "I want to be a fireman in the Marine Corps." And he's like, "Okay." So I signed on the dotted line. Sometime between boot camp and school training, the whole thing changed. They sent me to SOI, the School of Infantry, to train as a grunt. From then on, I was straight infantry. I never did get to go to firefighting school. I don't know what I thought. I thought my orders got changed somehow. Later I found out that my recruiter did some bad things. Like some people who couldn't pass the aptitude test? He had people to take it for them. He made some fake high school diplomas for some guys to join. It took the Marine Corps a while to figure that out. Finally, they caught him. He's out now. But what happened with me was, after I was in for three years—I'd been to Spain, Iraq, Afghanistan—they gave me a choice: Either you can get out of the Marines, or you can continue staying in. If I wanted to stay in, I would have to stay infantry. I was like, "You know what? Lemme switch jobs, 'cause I already did enough infantry jobs. Let me become a fireman like he promised in the first place." But they were like, "Nah, you don't get that choice. Either you stay infantry, or you get out." If I got out, see, it would be like they'd erase my name from the books, like I was never in the military at all. I wouldn't even be a veteran. All record of my service would be gone. I had worked way too hard for that. It had to do with the fact that my contract was forged or something, or because it was made under illegal circumstances or whatever. So I was like, okay, I got two years left. I'll just stay in.

The first time I ever got shot at was my first deployment to Iraq. This was 2003. We were in Nazarea. We'd cleared out the town, everything was fine. We were just waiting to go over the bridge—at the time, it was Saddam's regime over there across the river. We were dug in and waiting for a command to move. We had already put some vehicles over there, some tanks, and we were just waiting for the go ahead, getting ready to fire, getting ready to take over the city because it was gonna be a big battle, a big pain in the butt.

I was in my hole, you know, we were dug in, we had to dig a hole with our own little shovel. There was a sniper somewhere. Probably across the river. And he took a shot and it hit the tree behind me, it hit the bark, it just barely missed me. I heard the crack in the wind, just like this *craaaaack*, unmistakable, and then I heard it hit the tree right behind me. It must have gone, I don't know, like one inch over my head. If it had been one inch lower, or maybe two inches lower, I could have been dead. I have to tell you: I was boot. I was pretty scared. I stayed down on the ground for like thirty minutes. I didn't want to get up. I was shocked. I was like *Wow*, you know? Because the second that bullet whizzed over my head, it was like this moment for me, this moment where things came into sharp focus. Like *Snap!!*, you know? The first thing that went through my mind was the fact that my wife was pregnant. *My wife's pregnant! I gotta get down, because I'm coming home alive. I am coming home alive.* And then it was like, *Wow, I could have been dead just now. If I'd made the wrong movement and was in the path of the bullet, I could have been dead. If I had reached back to scratch my ass at that moment, and raised my head just a little bit while I was doing it, I could have been frickin' dead.* I was thinking all kinds of weird stuff like that. But then, at the same time, you still got that Marine Corps mentality in you. After all that, I got mad. I wanted to shoot this guy who was shooting at me, this guy who was fucking up my whole life, putting my life in danger. I wanted to kill this guy, because Marines don't retreat. They're not wussies, period. That's the reason why they call us Devil Dogs.

After our sniper took out their sniper, they called on the radio to say everything's clear. I got back up, and from then on, I was never standing still. I was always moving, walking in a square, moving around, never standing still so a sniper could shoot me. The Gunny was like, "*What* are you doing?" and I was like, "I don't wanna get shot, sir. My wife is six months pregnant."

That was my second deployment, January to May 2003. Then, four months later, I went to Afghanistan—August 2003 until February 2004. Then I went on a MEU—Saudi Arabia, Israel, Jordan, Kuwait, Iraq, Malta, Greece, Italy, Spain. That was July 2005 until January 2006. Then I re-enlisted and I went to DI school. I wanted to be a drill instructor. Unfortunately, I hurt my wrist in DI school and had to quit. I went back to Iraq in July 2006—as a grunt.

When I got back to Iraq, it was weird. Everything had totally changed. Nothing compared to this deployment, everything had gone to shit. It's horrible there. It's one hundred times worse. The Iraqi soldiers we're supposed to be working with? They get behind a wall, and they hold their weapons up over their heads, and they fire over the wall. They don't even aim. How the fuck do they expect to kill the enemy like that? They act like they're working with you, but they're just stabbing you in the back. They know who the bad guys are, but they're not helping us out. You can't trust them, so you just teach them the bare minimum. I don't teach them everything I know. No fuckin' way. Because they're gonna turn around one day and use it against you. You know how, in *our* military, you have to sign a contract for three or four years or whatever? If you're in the military, you're in for four years. No matter what. That's us. If we don't do what we're supposed to do, we go to jail and do hard time. But over there, if an Iraqi signs a contract, he can quit any time he wants. Like, when you're training these guys, if you piss someone off, guess what you just did? You just made a terrorist. You just created a terrorist. And then they'll go right to their terrorist buddies, and they'll be like, "Guess what? The Marines train like this, they do that, this is what they do." That's the reason we don't teach them everything we know. We just teach them the basics, so they can learn to take care of their country, so we can leave.

That's what I was doing when I was hit. I was training Iraqis. November 11, 2006, fourteen hundred hours, also known as 2:00 p.m. I was walking in the street in a city called Anah. It was me and my squad. We had the 2nd LAR with us, light armor reconnaissance. We were teaching the Iraqis an exercise where I basically show them what to do and what not to do on a patrol. And see, always, before I got out on patrol, I like to do what I call my "research." You have to understand: When I'm over there, I'm a nonstop person. They call me Lightswitch. That's another of my nicknames. Lightswitch. I'm either on, or I'm off. I'm off when I'm in the States. But if it's time to train, or if I'm in Iraq, the switch is on. And when that switch is on, it stays on until I leave that nasty place over there. So I'm always on guard. I'm always on the move. I'm always doing something, always keeping my guys busy, keeping 'em motivated. If there's a patrol, before we go, I'll go talk to the squad leader who just came in. I'll be like, "How did your patrol go? What did you guys find? What did you guys see? Anything suspicious? I'm always taking four or five steps before everybody takes a step. I'm always ahead of everybody. I'm always that person to be like, *All right, what can I do to make this better? What can I do to make it safer for my men?* See, when I'm over there, I'm always thinking. You have to be. Because the people, these Iraqis, they don't care. They'll do anything to hurt you. They'll put a bomb in a dog or a cow, whatever. They'll put a bomb in their cousin's body. They do that, you know, booby-trap dead bodies. They say it's all about religion over there. What kind of religion is it if it's okay to blow up your cousin's dead body? One minute you're just walking along on the street. The next minute, you're dead. Or you're hurt. That's how nasty those people are. You gotta learn to think like a terrorist. So that's what I do. If you can't beat 'em, join 'em, you know? You got to think like 'em. That's what I always tried to do.

So we're on patrol, we're walking down the street in Anah, and all of a sudden I spot this hole on the side of the street—something I didn't remember being there before. I was looking through my ACOG, advanced combat optical gun sight, which is like a sniper scope. It's mounted on the weapon. So I got my weapon pointed at this hole, where it's obvious that someone's been digging. And as I'm looking through the scope, just as I was about to yell out and say that I'd spotted this suspicious hole, before I even said the first two words, there was this huge *BOOM*.

Everything shook. Black smoke everywhere. I was still standing on my feet. I looked to my right, and Sergeant Holizinger was on the ground fifteen feet away from where he'd been one second ago. I was like, "Oh my goodness." I tried to walk toward him, but I took one step and fell to the ground. I couldn't feel anything from my waist down. And then, like, within about thirty or forty seconds, I started feeling this burning sensation in my legs. I was like *Ahhhhhhhhhhh!* I mean, I done a lot of damage to myself over time. I've been in a lot of pain. I broke stuff. Once I dislocated a finger playing basketball, and I popped it back into place myself. But this pain... I'd never felt anything like it. I kinda yelled. I definitely yelled. I yelled, "FUCK! SHIT!" I was cussin'.

Then I looked down. There was blood everywhere. I was like, "You motherfuckers got me, but you know what? You can't stop me!" And I'm laying there, still pointing my weapon out, holding it with one arm, looking for the bad guys, because they could be anywhere. But I couldn't shoot, you know, because you gotta have positive identification of a target to shoot.

My corpsman pulled me out of the road. I was still conscious, but I had a terrible headache. My head was just pounding, pounding, pounding, and then my ears were just ringing. My head hurt all over. Like, the vibration of that blast, it felt like my stomach was turned inside out. I wanted to piss and shit at the same time. I'm lucky I didn't piss and shit myself. Sometimes a blast will make you do that. Doc says to me, "You're going home, buddy." And I was like, "Can I look?" And he was like, "Don't look, trust me, you don't want to see." Because there was a big chunk of metal stuck in my shin of my left leg. It fractured the bone, the tibia, the fibia. I had a fractured femur also, and a torn femoral artery. There was shrapnel all over my body: my left ankle, my knee, my upper thigh, my right calf, my lower knee, my upper body. I was peppered, peppered meaning hit by a bunch of shrapnel. It just went everywhere. So I took his advice and didn't look down. The only thing I saw was this gash in my arm. I was like, *That is freakin' huge.* I could see my muscles moving inside. Blood was squirting into my face. I was like, *Ahhhhh!* You know? It was *nasty.* The corpsman was like, "Do you have morphine?" But I was like, "No, man. That shit makes my penis soft." That kind of made him laugh. I was trying to keep up the morale, you know. I was the squad leader. It was like, "I'll be okay. You guys gotta carry on."

Right now, I have a lot of nerve pain, that's the worst part. But the most *annoying* part is all the shrapnel. I can't sleep with sheets because the shit comes out of me while I'm sleeping. It gets snagged on the sheets and then of course it hurts. I have to have a space heater. I heat the air in the room real warm to counteract the air conditioning. I can't put a sheet or a blanket on myself. They call it migrating. The shrapnel migrates out of your body. It travels, it comes through the skin, like little tiny pebbles coming out. Or really, there's a variety of shapes and sizes. What you can do is you can be your own surgeon if you want. You can get a magnet and stick it next to your skin—if the magnet's strong enough, it'll pull it out. Once I put a magnet on my leg and it stuck to the shrapnel inside my body. It'll just stick right there. Everybody says it's pretty funny. A while back I flew home to Florida. I set off all the metal detectors. Luckily, they'd already called ahead and said I was coming. Everybody knew I was a wounded vet, so they treated me pretty well.

My morale has always been high. That's what I've always been known for. Being motivated. Being upbeat. That's one reason why I wanted to be a DI. I've always been a motivated guy. But lately, you know, there are days... I guess everybody has their days, right? If I'm having one of my days, I just stay away from everybody. Because my morale's not good, my attitude's not good, I'm in a bad mood. I'm infectious in a bad way. I don't know what it is. Maybe after I got bombed, I got more short-fused. Like I barely have enough patience for anything. I'm just so darn short-fused. Sometimes I go to WalMart. I go shopping and everything, I pick out what I want. But then, I get to the line and it's ridiculously long. And standing there waiting, I just lose my patience. I get pissed, you know? I can't stand there anymore. So I'll just drop everything and go walk outside and drive somewhere else. And then of course I'll have to shop all over again. That's one thing that happens to me. Or sometimes I get these random headaches. Once I have the random headache, I will not be downstairs at all—I will be sleeping in the bed the whole day. These are worse than migraines. It just pounds and pounds everywhere around the head. You don't want to do anything. You don't want to answer the door, you don't want to hear nobody knocking, you don't want to hear nobody at all. You don't want to be near nobody.

Basically, my contract says I get out on October 17, 2009. But I plan on getting out within the next year. The doctor says first I have to do about six months of therapy, which I have to wait a while to do, because basically the nerve damage is screwing me, and my legs are not healing the way we want them to heal, and they don't want to do any more operations, because they could cause even more nerve damage. So far, I've had three operations. So we're really just waiting to see if the nerves are gonna calm down a bit. I'm on a couple different medications to help that out. There's this dream I have. It's the same dream over and over. It's me walking down the street in Anah before I got blown up. And as I'm walking, as I'm looking through my ACOG, trying to get a closer look at that suspicious hole in the ground, I'm waiting for the boom to come. I know it's coming. I'm aware that I'm dreaming. I know that I'm in a dream. I keep telling myself, *Wake up. Wake up! Wake up before the bomb goes off!* Because every time I have this dream, the bomb goes off, and I get scared shitless and I wake up in this cold sweat. But it's always too late, I can't get myself to wake up. The bomb always goes off, *BOOOM!*

And then I wake up in a cold sweat, and there's this feeling inside of me. I say I'm scared shitless but really, it's not fear because I'm not scared of anything. It's more like anger. First comes the anger. Because we're over there in Iraq trying to help these people, but they don't wanna be helped. They're not telling us everything. They're screwing us over. They want us to die and get hurt. That's the first thing—anger. And then the second thing would be... well, my kids. I want to be around to help them grow up.

***

Friday afternoon formation. A lot of the guys haven't bothered to show up. Sergeant D has sent a fire team, three guys, to scout the dorm—to bang on doors and rouse the Devil Dogs from their naps or jerking off or whatever the fuck they're doing when they're supposed to be here.

Ringo, Cybula, and Leeman are here on time, sitting together on the doctor's-office chairs in their usual spot in the back of the room.

"The hardest thing to deal with when I got back," Ringo is saying, "Was the fact that my guys were still over there. I've been with my guys coming up on three years now. I know when their bowel movements are. I know 'em that well. I know what foods give 'em gas. Or why this guy is all of a sudden really angry for some reason. When you know people like that, and then suddenly you're gone, it's really tough."

"I think a lot of people think we come back and we're real happy we're home," Cybula says. "Yeah, we're glad we're alive. We're not stupid. But they don't see the other side of it."

"My thing is, it's warfare. People die. People you *know*," Ringo says. "The hardest thing I've ever done was at my buddy's memorial service. You put the helmet on top of the rifle, the boots in front. It was the hardest goddamn thing I've ever done in my life."

"I had no illusions about it goin' in," Cybula says. "I still don't."

"I don't complain about it, but it upsets me," says Ringo. "'Cause I got hit and had to leave my boys. Now I been six months with this thing, and I got no feeling in my hand."

"Ain't that good for jerkin' off?"

"Yeah, like it's somebody else with a weak grip."

"No matter how much you train to deal with stuff like that, it's still gonna be hard."

"People always think it'll happen to someone else," Leeman mumbles. He is not a man of many words, but when he says something, and you can understand it, it usually has the air of folksy wisdom.

"When that round went through my helmet," Ringo says, "I thought, *This was supposed to be the one that killed me.*"

"Well, it didn't, man," Leeman says conclusively.

"What do you know about that?" Ringo sings.

"It gets so bad over there," Cybula says. "At first, you're all, like, alert and lookin'. Scared shit, even though nobody admits it. By the time you get to that third month, it's like you actually *like* it. You get to that point where you need that adrenaline rush. And then you come back here, and everything is so damn slow. You're still lookin' for that rush. You come back here, and you try to fit back into your life, but it don't work. Your relationships with everybody suck. They don't understand how you feel."

"I came back, and my wife was like, 'I'm not sure you've dealt with your issues,'" Ringo says, doing an impression of an Oprah-influenced female. "And I'm like, 'Yeah, no *shit*. I lost half my platoon when I was over there. I didn't really have no time to deal with it. I think I was a little busy, doing my job, *trying to keep my boys alive*. I waited until I got home to deal with shit."

"The women just want you to come home and take care of their problems," Leeman says.

"Big daddy's home," Ringo sings, another tune.

"Everybody here helps everybody else out," Cybula says. "We're here with other people who share the same problems with you. You're not alone. If me and him were back in our unit, you know, on LIM DU, whatever, the whole grunt mentality is like 'Oh yeah, you're a wuss, you're not doing your job, you're just sitting around the barracks fakin' like you're hurt.' So they send us here, and it's like a fair mentality. Everybody else is hurt too. Your job is to get better."

"Here's something you can record," Ringo says. "After I went to that funeral in Arlington—for the young Marine I tried to help? Me and my younger brother, who is also a Marine, we go to the Marine Corps Museum. We're standing there looking at these photos of the landing on Iwo Jima, and these two ladies are there also. The pictures are pretty graphic. You see Marines jumping off the side of the boat and people getting hit. And the ladies, they're like, 'Man, it takes a lot of courage to do what you guys do.' And when she said that, I don't know, something just hit me real quick, and I'm like, 'No ma'am, it ain't courage. It's love.' That's what I told her. Because it ain't courage. What we do is not courage. It's love. It's love for the guys. Like I always say, this is as close as you can be to a man without being gay. There's no such thing as courage in the Corps, it's all about love."

"I would *love* to be in a firefight *right now*," Cybula says. "I would absolutely love *that*. It would make my day. Remember the kill house we found in Fallujah? They were like, takin' people's eyeballs out, torturing people every way they could, fuckin' stretching 'em out and stuff like that. These were Iraqis doing it to their own Iraqi people. Remember that, Ringo?"

Ringo cuts his eyes toward his former suitemate. "I never been to Fallujah, bro."

***

Sergeant D is really pissed. It's 3:30 p.m. He's still here. He could have dismissed these guys an hour ago if they'd shown up. It's Friday, true, and all the senior guys have left for Myrtle Beach to play golf, but where the fuck is the military discipline? They are still Marines. He scratches his head. His skull is caved in slightly on the right front, above his eyebrow.

Jack Durgala, Jr. is thirty-one, from Birmingham, New York. He actually met his father for the first time courtesy of the U.S. Marines. His buddy was working as a recruiter. He was on a call at a family's house to talk to their son, who wanted in. He noticed the name of the father, Jack Durgala, and asked if he knew his buddy, Sergeant D. The guy was like, "I've been looking for him for years."

Sergeant D was also training Iraqi soldiers when he got hit—a suspicious rice bag 200 feet down the road turned out to be an IED. His left leg was broken. His left foot got spun around. A piece of shrapnel hit the lower part of his right leg and took a big hunk out of it. Another piece ruptured his intestines. A piece of iron rebar embedded itself into his helmet. Luckily, he had one of the new-model helmets. Whoever designed it did a great job. The rebar hit the helmet and stuck, but it didn't go through. The force of the blow, however, was enough to split open his skull.

Like the others, Sergeant D's life was saved by quick work in the field and by quick evacuation. Combat mortality rates have fallen from 24 percent in Vietnam to 10 percent in Iraq and Afghanistan. Most troops are in Germany within a few days of their injury. They're back stateside within a week, two tops. Sergeant D has less intestine now than he used to. "Food goes through me a little bit faster," he laughs. He has nerve damage in his right leg: it causes something called drop foot. His left leg has metal plates and screws holding the foot to the ankle. He has very mild TBI, mostly a short-term-memory problem. Sometimes he'll tell his Marines to do the same thing five times, because he doesn't remember the other four. The worst for him is the nerve problem. "You know how when your leg falls asleep and you get the pins? Well," he says dryly, "I have the pins. Now dump gasoline on it, light it on fire, have a midget come over with a sledgehammer and start slamming on your foot, and then you add one deranged person with an ice pick trying to put the fire out, and then somebody coming by with water, ice-cold water, and dumping it on your leg. All that within a second. It just gets very frustrating, to say the least. And now they've diagnosed me with a crack in one of my vertebras from getting thrown by the blast. Every time I go to the doctor, it's something else. I'm happy that they found the problem, but I would like to move on with my life already.

"More or less, Maxwell Hall is kind of—" He searches for the right word. "A holding pen is the best way to put it. Some of the Marines refer to it as purgatory. A lot of the injuries they don't know how to fix. They don't know *what* to do. The gear is better now than before. If I was wearing, like, Vietnam-era gear, I wouldn't be alive right now. Today, more people are getting injured and living, and the doctors don't know how to solve a lot of the problems, especially the brain problems. Or like myself, nerve damage. Before, it was like, okay, the leg got ripped off, give him a prosthetic. Now, they reattach it. But how do you fix a nerve problem? Obviously, they don't know how."

Finally, some stragglers arrive in the rec room. Their numbers are obviously down from the morning formation. The place has the feel of a ghost town. It's something they're constantly struggling with in Maxwell Hall: how appropriate it is to still play the game.

"Every one of you in here should be frickin' pissed off at the guys that aren't at formation," Sergeant D tells them, pacing the floor in front of them. "'Cause you been waiting around for an extra hour while we're trying to track everybody down. Simple shit. You know it's Friday. You know we're gonna get the hell outta here as early as I can get us outta here, right? So get your frickin' buddies, your roommates, whatever, get 'em to start doing what you're supposed to be doing. It's simple. All you gotta do is show up. Nobody's making you frickin' fill sandbags or anything like that. Nobody's being abused. As far I'm concerned, this is the best barracks I've ever seen. Yes, it sucks, the reason why you came here, I ain't arguing that. Just do what the fuck you gotta do to get yourself better to go back to your unit, to medically retire, to get your money every month, or whatever.

"I mean, I walked through the barracks today, and let me put it this way: I'm embarrassed as fuck about the whole fuckin' barracks. Some of those rooms I walked in.... If Sergeant Simms wasn't standing there next to me at the door, restraining me—just about physically restraining me, that was what it was coming down to—I would have dumped every piece of shit in those rooms. *Everything* would have been on the floor. You would be lost in laundry like fuckin' Hurricane Katrina. Only this would have been Hurricane D. Don't let me find your fuckin' rooms like I found them today. Vacuum your damn floors. Pick up your goddam dirty laundry. I don't care if you gotta do a goddam sniff test, you do it. If it stinks, throw it in the wash. Get yourself a laundry hamper or something. Get a laundry bag. Put your shit away. You got food and shit in your room, fuckin' put it in the goddam fridge. Don't just leave it sittin' the fuck out. We had a real bad problem with ants last year. Let's not give the ants any fuckin' reason to come in. Tupperware works pretty goddam good, gentlemen. You just stick it in your microwave. And the fuckin' toilets. Holy fuck! Holy FUCK! A disaster within itself. Gentlemen: They sell this thing at WalMart for like ninety-nine cents. This little scrubby thing? Buy one. Rub it around in there. It's an amazing piece of technology. You should look into it. If you don't wanna do that, you can fuckin' stick your hand down there like a fuckin' ape and scrub away. Whatever. I DO NOT WANT TO SEE THE TOILETS LOOKING THAT WAY ANYMORE.

"Let's get out there and start doing what we're supposed to do. It's simple. Get a haircut. Wash your uniform once in a while. Some of y'all stink, all right? I got a girlfriend. She washes my shit. If you can't get a girlfriend, then get a boyfriend and have him wash your shit, all right? Wash your uniform, get a haircut, clean out your room. Clean the frickin' toilets. Take care of yourself. If you got a problem, don't wait until it becomes a huge problem to let somebody know about it. If you don't feel comfortable talking to a squad leader, come talk to me. If you don't wanna talk to 'em, go talk to Master Sergeant Barnes. Go talk to the doc. Tell me you wanna see your chaplain. *Whatever.* If you're having sad thoughts or bad thoughts or family problems or something, everybody in here's got something going on in their head—whether you realize it yet or not, something's going on up there. And if you've got other problems, that's just gonna escalate things. So talk to somebody, okay?

"Besides all that, do all the right things for the right reasons this weekend. No drinkin' and drivin'. If it ain't eighteen, don't fuck it. If it is, wear a condom."

"Errrr," the Devil Dogs chorus.

***

Brandy and Jeff Leeman are sitting side by side on the floral couch in their little two-bedroom house, about ten minutes across base from Maxwell Hall. Presently off duty, Corporal Leeman is wearing civvies—tee shirt and blue jeans. In this getup, he looks a lot less like a grizzled Marine veteran and a lot more like what he also is—one year out of his teenage years, the same age as most college juniors. The furnishings in the house have a newlywed feel: the DVD collection, the shot glass and beer mug collection, the framed certificate from the "Before I Do" Marriage Foundation Workshop. There is a computer desk at one end of the living room, an entertainment center on the other. Brandy bought the latter with her employee discount at Target while her husband was in Iraq. She assembled it herself. It took six hours.

On Leeman's lap sits Gunner, their miniature Doberman Pinscher. Gunner has a lame leg like his master—his right hind. He was born that way. He'll sit on Leeman's lap all day long if he's allowed. Gunner has this weird thing where he doesn't want anyone to be in the bathroom without him. If you go in to poop and you close the door, Brandy explains, Gunner will put up this huge ruckus until he's let in—turns out he just wants to sit there and observe. Brandy is wearing a red t-shirt with the word Marines in yellow script across the area of her body we're not allowed to mention on tape. In her lap, she holds Lucky, a shepherd mutt they found in a ditch on the side of the road, starving and full of fleas. Lucky, indeed. This is their little family.

"All they do is show the bad shit," Leeman is saying. He is talking about the press, the nightly news, the impressions people have of the war in Iraq. "They don't show how we help the little kids. How we give them food and stuff, even though some of them might be wired up with IEDs—did Kinnee ever tell you this story about the kid? The press doesn't show the kind of stuff we see. They don't show how all the Iraqis get their water out of the Euphrates River—where they put all their waste. They take a dump in there, they put all their pollution in there, and then they go and get the same water to drink. You don't see reports on how we're building up the water treatment plants over there so that the people aren't nasty and disgusting all the time. And how we're giving them actual food instead of them having to go out and catch fish and grow stuff. The press shows us doing bad things. But what they don't show is, like, say we accidentally kick in the wrong door or something like that? Say we're on a patrol or we're looking for bad guys, and we kick in the wrong door. I bet you didn't know that the U.S. government will pay to have that door fixed. We will *pay* to have it fixed. They don't show that. They show us kicking it in, and the Iraqis getting mad about it, but they don't show us paying to fix it."

"If I was over there, I'd keep my happy little butt in the tent," Brandy says. She is fair and freckled, with long, straight, naturally red hair. When her husband was in Iraq, she sent him packages several times a week. At the FOB, he slept on an AeroBed until it mysteriously got stabbed. He ate so much junk food, he gained twenty pounds. Her packages continue to arrive since his return, rerouted back from Iraq—there were some crumbled homemade cookies in the last box. What Leeman really missed while he was over there (besides his favorite unmentionables, of course) was Brandy's lasagna. Whenever she makes it for dinner, his buddies from Maxwell Hall start showing up.

"When you're over there," Leeman explains, "You do what you're *told*."

"That's what you signed up for, right?"

"Is *that* what I signed up for?" he laughs. "Why *did* I sign up, anyways?"

"Because you didn't want to go to college?"

"Where I probably would have just flunked out and wasted a bunch of time and money."

"And because it was a way to keep you out of trouble back home."

"Most of my buddies from back then are working on a farm now. Or they're in the military. Ninety percent of my class went into the military."

"Or they went to jail."

"There's that. I wasn't ever in no trouble with the law, but maybe I woulda been."

"Lebanon, Tennessee," Brandy says. As if the name is explanation enough.

"And now I want to go back."

"Back to Lebanon?"

"Back to Iraq."

"Back to Iraq," she repeats. There is an odd tone in her voice, neither upbeat nor down.

"When I got hit, I didn't want to go home. I didn't want them to send me home."

"You were kind of excited about coming home, but at the same time you were upset. The first couple of weeks, you were like, 'Man, I wish I was back over there.' And I was like, 'Why would you want to go back over there?' And you're like, 'My friends are still over there, and I want to help them.'"

"I'm still trying to get back to active duty," Leeman says. "My old captain? He's moved over to H&S Company. He's pretty much telling me he can get me back, and I can be on light duty till I get out. That means I can go to Iraq and *everything*."

"What do you mean, 'till you get out?'"

"Well, I get out next November, so if I stay on light duty until—"

"I don't want you to get out. I want you to re-enlist."

"I do too, babe."

She looks at him. "It's job security, right? It would be rough if you get out and neither of us has a job and neither of us has been to college. And then we'll have to move back home, and I'll have to give up my job here at the dealership, and you won't have a job. I guess you could probably go home and work on the police force like your stepdad."

"The Marines is job security," Leeman agrees, nodding with all the sagacity of someone who has experienced life on this earth for nearly two decades. When he was growing up, his mom was always working. She used to be a nurse; now she sells construction equipment. His dad was a landscaper. They were divorced when he was twelve or thirteen. His stepdad used to sell medical equipment; now he's on the police force, working as a guard at the jail. Brandy's dad used to work for Nissan, building cars at a plant in Smyrna, Tennessee; her stepmom is a registered nurse. (There is a big nursing school at a nearby college.) Brandy's bio-mom only recently came back into her life. She works as a cashier at a gas station-convenience store. Her stepdad works in a pencil factory.

Brandy scratches Lucky vigorously behind the ears. The first time she saw Leeman at church, she thought he was hot, but there was *no way* she was going to talk to him. She was just standing there, like *Wow*, you know? But she wasn't going to say anything to anybody, because she didn't want anybody to tell him. It was, after all, a very small church in a very small town. Three pews, an aisle down the middle. Everybody knew everybody's business. Leeman was new. Brandy was like *Oh God, this is gonna be horrible. He's not gonna like me.* And then her stepbrother gets this big smirk on his face. "You can't go out with *him*," he tells her. And she was like, "Who said I wanted to go out with *him*?" but secretly she was thinking, *Oh God! He knows! How does he know? Is it that obvious?* That was almost three years ago now.

"Of course, if you stay in, I'll be worried the whole time that you'll get hurt again," Brandy says. "After *hurt*, there's only one more thing that can happen."

Leeman cocks an eyebrow, devil-may-care. "If I was gonna be dead, wouldn't I be dead already?"

"When you called me from the hospital—"

"I was high as a kite on morphine."

"It was 10:00 in the morning. I had just got home from working all night at Target. We were getting the Christmas stuff done, like we had to put all the display trees together, and we had to redo the toy section. I had just got home and I was getting ready to lay down, and I think I was eating because I remember I was starving, and then my phone rings and I look at the display and I'm like, *Okay, it's a weird number, it's gotta be him.* So I answer and I'm like, 'Hey, how you doing?' And you're like—"

"I don't even remember what I said." His lips curl, a rakish smile. He plays tom-tom with his fingertips on Gunner's smooth belly.

"I *remember*," Brandy says. "You said you was in the hospital at Al Asad. And I was like, 'WHAT ARE YOU DOING IN THE HOSPITAL AT AL ASAD!!!!?'"

"When you're over there, you can't think about getting injured, or you're not gonna be doing your job," Leeman says. "If you're worrying, you're letting your guy to the left and right down. You're going to get them hurt or yourself hurt. When somebody gets hurt in Iraq, you say, 'That sucks.' But you can't really think about it—on patrols and stuff you can't really think about it. Otherwise, you're gonna screw yourself and everybody else. It gets infectious. It's juju. The deployment's gonna be miserable."

"Aren't you afraid to get..." She searches for the right words. "Hurt again?"

He shrugs. His face rearranges itself into a somewhat abashed expression, maybe something like a fraternity brother who is about to tell his fiancée some secrets. "Everybody is afraid. A little. But they'd rather just go over there and deal with it instead of worrying about it the rest of their lives. You know how they say—shoulda, coulda, woulda. You don't wanna have that."

Brandy nods seriously, taking it in.

"And besides," Leeman continues, "going back over there a

second time—it's gotta be different. It's like doing anything the second time. I've already been hurt. I know what to do. I know the drill. I know what the processes are now, so it won't be as bad if I'm hurt again."

He looks at her. She looks at him. Neither seems convinced.

***

On Sunday afternoon, the old man is wearing cargo shorts. His feet are bare—the ghosts of socks meet the tan lines on his rock-solid calves. The founder of Maxwell Hall is sitting in a cheap, plastic patio chair—three for five dollars at the CVS—on the narrow front porch of his house, in a well-laid-out development behind the strip malls of greater Jacksonville. There is a man-made lake with a fountain, a rec area with fields and courts, a water tower presiding over rows, and cul-de-sacs of cute little houses made of siding and stucco in several styles.

On that fateful day three years ago, Lieutenant Colonel Tim Maxwell—Max to his friends, a graduate of Texas A&M, father of two, triathlete, career leatherneck on his sixth deployment, operations officer for the 4th Marine Expeditionary Unit—walked back to his tent in the seemingly secure command compound after lunch at the chow hall and prepared to take a fifteen-minute power nap. He took off his flak vest and his helmet. He left his boots on. He was dirty and dusty, so he lied down on the wooden floor of the tent (or maybe he lied down on his bed; another thing he can't remember clearly). It is interesting how fast you can crash out, he says, snapping his fingers. Comfort is irrelevant when you're exhausted. You just lie down and turn it off.

He was in a secure area, the command base. His tent was secured all around with, with—that stuff in the bag. What's the word? Not concrete... you fill them up... they're heavy... *sandbags*. There were sandbags leading out the door of the tent, an alley of sandbags, like a tunnel without a roof, two feet wide, six feet high. The alley ran for about three feet, then turned a hard left, continued on for a bit. He hadn't been asleep for more than five minutes, ten at most, when enemy mortars hit the compound. There would be about fifteen in all. The first one landed right in the middle of Maxwell's sandbag alley, just outside the flap of his tent.

Two pieces of shrapnel entered his brain through his left cheek near the zygomatic arch. The fragments damaged the central and temporal areas of his brain on the left, and also the optic radiation on the left. Specifically, the Broca and Wernicke's areas and possibly the conduction bundle between them were affected. This is where the language center of the brain is located. Because of the damage, Maxwell has expressive aphasia (trouble getting words out, problems with names and labels) and some receptive aphasia (trouble processing complex speech). The optic radiation damage left Maxwell with a right peripheral cut in both eyes, meaning that he can see to the left with both eyes but not to the right, despite having 20/25 vision. The shrapnel also damaged the motor portion of his brain, resulting in weakness and loss of control on the right side of his body, including his leg, arm, and face. Two mortar fragments are still embedded inside his brain, too deep to risk extraction. For three months, to allow his brain to heal, part of his skull was removed and placed inside his gut for safe keeping. More recently, surgeons have begun using acrylic to replace portions of the skull, cutting down the incidence of infection. For the most part, Maxwell's health and function have continued to improve, though he's had some problems during the past year with seizures. And then there are the pesky "crashes," as he likes to call them, when his brain gets overworked and overstimulated and shuts down. The doctors have been adjusting his meds. They'll just have to wait and see.

From the backyard can be heard shrieks and laughter, a small tenth birthday party for Maxwell's son, Eric, who always wears camo cargo shorts and wants to be a Marine when he grows up. He was six when his dad came home wearing a crash helmet to protect his injured brain where the piece of skull had been removed; he still worries that his dad might die unexpectedly in the middle of the night. Eric's best friend Collin is here, as is his thirteen-year-old sister, Alexis, and a contingent of rugrats, all of them cousins and neighbor kids, the children of Shannon Maxwell's sister and her two best friends, who together have formed their own little Marine wives support group, *Sex and the City* meets *Semper Fi*. Inside the planked fence, the yard is a patchwork quilt of mismatched sod—a large square of fescue here, Bermuda grass there, and over by the deck, an irregular weedy-looking rectangle of God-knows-what that Shannon picked up on sale at Home Depot while he was in Iraq. In one corner is a largish jumpy with a basketball hoop. In typical fashion, Shannon transported, dragged, and inflated it herself.

The daughter of an Air Force pilot who left active service when she was five, the former Shannon Grothues grew up in San Antonio, Texas, romanticizing about travel. "I hated not being the typical military brat," she says. As it happened, in twenty years as a Marine wife, she has never had the opportunity to live outside the continental United States, either. The couple met in College Station, Texas, when both were students at Texas A&M. He was an ROTC cadet; she was a business administration major, with an emphasis on marketing and advertising. The setting was a dive bar called the Dixie Chicken, an Aggie hangout. Shannon was nursing a beer, watching TV while her roommate and another friend were playing pool with some of Maxwell's friends. Then Max walked in. Another pool table was open. He challenged her to a game. His eyes were very big and very blue.

Shannon liked his confidence. She liked his broad shoulders. She liked—well, she doesn't know how to put it into words without sounding like the kind of woman she's not. Bottom line, he's probably a lot like her father. A very strong individual, but also an individual who listens and respects her opinions and her ideas. Maxwell graduated in May, 1989; they were married in July. She graduated the following June, after only three years. Maxwell took five years to graduate—let's just say his freshman year wasn't all about academics. He likes to joke that between them, they averaged four years a degree. For the record, each took two years to earn their masters.

As Maxwell pursued his career as a first lieutenant at Camp Pendleton, Shannon worked as a junior executive at an ad agency in Orange County. Most of his friends were not married; Shannon was the only wife in the group. They had a great time going to bars and picking out women for the boys. They'd do Thanksgiving dinners at their house, that was fun too. They purposely didn't live on base—Shannon didn't feel like she had a lot in common with the other Marine wives. They were all very much into their husbands' careers; they had kind of taken their husbands' identities. Shannon saw her marriage as a collaboration between two strong people with bright futures ahead. When Tim was gone on deployment, though she missed him, it kind of worked in her favor. She stayed late at the office. Ten p.m. was not unusual. Her bosses loved her. After their two children were born, Shannon quit working full time. Over the years, she has earned a first-degree black belt in Tae Kwon Do, taught martial arts to four and five year olds, created and supervised a practice for a popular psychiatrist, earned a master's degree in international management and marketing, ran the Marine Corps Marathon. More recently, she started Hope for the Warriors with her good friend Robin Kelleher, which helps spouses and families of wounded Marines, providing everything from food, groceries, and fishing rods to rental cars for moms and dads and lodging for "morale visits" from spouses. Last spring, in a White House ceremony, President Bush presented Shannon with an award for her efforts.

"I don't think, when I was twenty years old, I really comprehended what was at stake, what he was really going to be doing for a living," Shannon says. "As I got older and he started commanding Marines, I started understanding the magnitude of it all, the huge responsibility that was resting on his shoulders. The fact that he's got to be responsible for the lives of these young men—that they're going to be in harm's way and that he's responsible for them—that is a huge thing, a huge responsibility, to have people's lives in your hands. It's not until you're a parent that you really understand. Each one of these Devil Dogs is somebody's baby.

"When your husband goes to war, you worry about a lot of facets. Before a deployment, the worst part of our preparation is always having to talk about, okay, 'What are your wishes? What do you want done?' Basically, you prepare yourself, you envision what the kids and I are going to do if the worst thing happens. Self-defense teaches you that also—to run through all the scenarios in your head so you'll know how to react when the time comes. To a certain extent, after twenty years, it's something that you've reconciled. He might be killed. You've told yourself that a million times. The weird thing is, I wasn't really prepared for him to be injured. For some reason, I never really considered *that* scenario. I don't know why.

"When I got the call, the first thing that went through my mind was just, *Okay. He's not dead. We can get through this.* As time goes on you learn what you have to learn. You learn about the injuries. You learn about the drugs and the therapy. You learn about doctors and hospitals. You have to become your own best medical advocate. And you learn humility. When he was in the VA hospital in Richmond, they were calling him Mr. Maxwell for the first time in his life. It was such a loss of identity. It was humbling.

"Things are more different now than I would ever have envisioned," Shannon says. "But it's not worth crying about it or worrying about. You have to live for the moment. You make the best of it. Especially with kids, you have to do that, because they have enough concerns at their age. I grew up living in a very strong and determined family. You accomplish challenges. You attack them and you get through them and grow because of them."

The Maxwells have lived in this house for four years; there is a bittersweet feeling to the birthday proceedings. Tim is leaving in a couple of days for Quantico. The family will follow soon. They have to pack up, buy a new house, sell this one, find new schools, new soccer and softball teams, new everything. Of course, the move is a sign that Maxwell is healing, moving forward, contributing. Perhaps he is not the same man he set out to be, but who knows: Had he not lost some of himself in Iraq, would he ever have contributed as much as he has?

"I use my story all the time in hospitals, when I'm visiting the wounded," Maxwell says. "I tell them about good luck and bad luck.

I tell them about how I got blown up in an area that was supposedly secure. Come on? What's the odds of that?

"The thing is," he says, his thick hands set earnestly upon his khaki-clad thighs, his voice small and conspiratorial, "I never even fired my frickin' weapon at anybody when I was over there. Never. Not in twenty years. I'm not happy about that, but I'm okay with it. It is how it is."

He looks out across the yard. One neighbor is blowing grass cuttings off his driveway, another is trimming a hedge—the little two-stroke engines rev and whine in harmony. A bunch of kids are playing pirate in a trailered fishing boat; a couple of teenage goth boys on ridiculously small bicycles pedal past, trailing attitude. "Some of these young Marines, they have a lot of mixed feelings when they get back," Maxwell says. "Like Kinnee. He got injured after only three months of combat. He didn't have no firefights. He feels like a pussy. I tell 'em, 'Hey, look at me.' I've had six pumps, three of 'em in a combat zone. But I'm always in a platoon that never gets no action. When people call me a hero, how do you think I feel? Don't call me no hero. What did I do?"

He tilts back in the chair, the hind legs wrinkle and wobble owing to the cheap material, a little taste of danger he seems to enjoy. He sets his eyes to the horizon, to the place where the tall and lush green trees become the glinty gray sky, which is heavy with the portent of another summer shower. His ice-blue eyes reflect his determination. The awkward cast of his face, the slight lag on the right side, lends him an air of bewilderment. There are big changes in the offing. He has no idea what lies ahead. He has no idea if he is up to the challenge. In private moments, frankly, he is damned concerned.

But he's been trained to put one foot in front of the other. That is what he will do. He will move to Quantico. He will work for the new regiment. He will continue to help wounded Marines. He will try to be of use.

***

At zero five thirty hours, the first floor of Maxwell Hall is deserted. The only sound is the hum of the fluorescent lighting. Lance Corporal Robert J. Wild is pulling watch at the fitness center. He sits in an office chair behind a typical front desk. Before him is an array of treadmills and ellipticals and other workout machines, TVs hanging from the ceilings, tuned to FOX News. His elbow rests on the Formica counter; his palm supports his chin. He stares out the window into the gathering dawn, the brick building across the way, the muddy waters of the New River shrouded in fog. Blond and boyishly handsome, he brings to mind a smaller, slighter version of the actor Brad Pitt—Brad's younger brother, perhaps, playing a skateboard dude from Moline, Illinois, who lived in a lot of foster homes before joining the Marines at seventeen.

"I forgot you were coming," he says to me, flashing his endearing smile. His nickname is Wildman. The tone of his voice is flat and matter-of-fact. "I can't remember nothin'. That's why I love this Palm Pilot. To remind me of my fuckin' appointments. Only sometimes I forget to program them in."

His eyebrows rise; his face registers something between concern and puzzlement. "I was only there for four months. I got back November 1. I've been married since February—six months. It was a quickie thing. I went out to a club and met her; I've always had this attraction for older women. She's thirty-eight. It was weird at first 'cause she has four kids. Her son is twenty and her daughters are nineteen, seventeen, and fifteen, and the nineteen-year-old is pregnant. She just got married to a Marine also. The seventeen-year-old is pregnant too. Her man just joined the army. My wife's son used to be a pro skateboarder, but now he does vinyl siding. My wife is a doctor. She works at Greenville Memorial hospital. She's a respiratory therapist. I didn't even know that until we'd been dating for a while. Before that I—"

The words come bubbling out of him. You get the impression that what he is saying is unfiltered truth, inside stuff gurgling to the surface like sweet water from a small natural spring. I ask him the proper spelling of his name. I ask him his birth date. It turns out to be today, July 13. He is twenty-two years old.

"Friday the thirteenth," he notes, as if it is evidence of something, as if it happens every year the same way.

I ask the date of his injury.

"There's this religious belief that the Hajis have, it's called Ramadan," he says, pulling the little stylus off of his Palm Pilot to keep his hands busy. "It's forty days and forty nights where they don't eat or drink anything during the daytime. They fast because they believe that if they do this, when they go to heaven, they'll be granted forty virgins, something like that. And they have this one day at the end of Ramadan, I forget what it's called, but it's a special day, a day when they show their faith to their God or their leader or whoever by attacking us. If they die on that day, they'll get that stuff in heaven, the virgins and stuff. That was the day I got whacked: October 19 of '06. Me and my buddy Dam Semrau were in a four-by-four post on top of a building. We got hit by a rocket-propelled grenade. I got thrown head-first into a wall. I injured my C spine and tore all the ligaments in my neck. I was in a neck brace for, like, four months.

"Now I can't think too well," he continues, replacing the stylus, picking up his phone, opening it to check for messages. "Like before, I was really active, and I wanted to do everything. Now I don't do the things I used to do. The main problem is my frontal lobe. It's not functioning. Frontal lobes. There are two. When you look at them on these tests, there's no activity. It's where you get your personality and your emotions and all kinds of stuff. Short-term things I can't remember. I can remember old stuff. Or if I repeat something enough to make it long-term, then I can remember it. Like people's names, I can't remember. I had trouble remembering my wife's name for a long time. It's hard, because it makes you feel like you're stupid. People don't understand what your problem is. You seem perfectly normal. They look at you funny. They don't understand that you've been blown up. So all they do is judge you.

"Before, I was really fun. I'm not much of anything anymore. Like, I used to like to do hobbies. I used to like to play sports. I used to love to weigh lift. I loved to draw and build things. I actually went to school for two years to be a carpenter. In school I did woodworking. I built an entertainment center, a couple of shelves, stuff like that. It was fun, because I know that I made this, and now somebody wants to buy it from me. It makes you feel good. The funnest thing was building houses. I once built a 2,000-square-foot house for a foster family. I was a foster kid for a long time because my mom couldn't keep me. Later we got back together. Before I went in the Marines, I got to live with her again. My mom works at Ryan's Steakhouse as a baker. My stepdad's name is Reggie Baker. Well, he's not really my stepdad because they're not married, but he's the closest thing I ever had to a dad. My real father was in the Marines, too. He got kicked out for selling cocaine and dealing drugs and doing other stuff. My family's pretty, like, low on the totem pole. Like, we have no rich relatives, no wealthy relatives, we're all pretty, you know, standard living. And everybody thought because I was a little problem child that I was going to turn out to be like my father, and that's the last thing I wanted. I wanted to join the Marines to prove to myself and to my family that I'm not, you know, that I'm gonna be better than him. And I already did more in six months on this deployment than my whole family has ever done in their whole lives. Like, I was the best driver in the battalion. My nickname was Ricky Bobby from that comedy movie. That name came directly from the CO. I was the driver of the lead truck. I never, ever got my crew blown up, not even one time."

Wildman reaches over and grabs a remote control. He aims it at the nearest television, begins flipping the channels. He settles on ESPN. All the rest of the monitors stay on FOX News.

"Now I'm depressed," he says. "It's affecting my marriage. It's affected my, you know, my friends, because I just have real bad anger problems. I guess I'm a little frustrated, a little mad. Like, the other day, in the rec room, I got bitched out for not vacuuming or something, and I just flipped out. I mean, I don't even live in the barracks, I live with my wife. But whenever I'm here, I usually take the initiative and clean up, so that way we can get dismissed early. And usually everybody else just sits around. This time I had a fuckin' killer headache, and I just didn't feel like cleaning up. And this guy's all up my ass about why didn't I vacuum. And I just

flipped out, I was like, 'What? Are you talking to me? DO I HAVE
BITCH WRITTEN ACROSS MY FOREHEAD!?!'

"I guess I'm just tired of the Marine Corps. It's nobody's fault.
It was good for me before—until I got messed up. Right now, I
couldn't even go to college and learn anything, because my brain
isn't functioning enough to where I could remember what you
taught me yesterday."

He pulls a Newport cigarette out of the package, gestures
toward the door. We walk outside, take a seat on the concrete steps.

He lights up, drags deeply. "It kinda makes you feel like a
failure," he says.

"Why?" I ask.

"Because you signed a contract, but you couldn't do your four
years. You couldn't do your job."

"But you got blown up. it's not like you went AWOL or
something."

"It's not what you picture when you sign up."

"I guess if you did, you wouldn't sign up in the first place."

"Young, dumb, full of cum."

"That's what they say."

"I can't remember half the time what I ate yesterday, or what
I had a conversation about ten minutes ago. I'm always, like, trying
real hard to think."

"Don't you feel like there's been any improvement at all?"

"No."

"Not any?

"I think it's getting worse."

I look at this kid. It's his birthday. I don't know what to say.
Dawn is breaking, but it's too cloudy to see the sun rising over the
river. The air is damp and cool, that time of day people always say
makes them feel hopeful, full of possibility. I put my hand on his
shoulder and squeeze, and then I pat his back a few times—hard,
manly pats, like you'd do with a big, friendly dog.

Wildman takes another deep drag of his Newport. He looks at
me with his Brad Pitt eyes. "It's cool, bro, don't worry about it. It's
a normal thing for me."

Vetville

More than 2 million Americans have served in
the Afghanistan and Iraq wars. Many returned
wounded, thousands have committed suicide—
nearly 25 percent suffer from PTSD or major
depression with little hope of relief. On one small
farm in the mountains of Tennessee, Alan Beaty
and his ragtag squad of Marine vets have found a
modest solution—taking care of each other.

A lan Beaty navigates a rutted road, once again a man on a mission.
His eyes track grimly side to side, scanning for irregularities
along this dusty and familiar route in the Cumberland Mountains
of Tennessee. Gravel ricochets off the undercarriage of his battered
red Honda CR-V, the springs squeak and complain. The half-assed
mini-crossover van is a remnant of his former life, when he was a
postmaster and a husband, a full-time father; he'd found it parked
outside his empty house upon his return from his third tour in
Iraq. The odometer has already run around twice. It will have to do.
There is no room in the budget for a car payment—inevitably he
finds himself finishing out the month on·pimento cheese, Wonder
Bread, and moonshine, brewed in a 150-year-old still rescued from
the family homestead, awarded to his great-great-great-great-
grandfather for his service in the Revolutionary War, at the Battle
of Kings Mountain.

Andrew Beaty walked hundreds of miles in 1780 to lend his long rifle to this pivotal victory in the fight for American independence; history records him as one of the original Overmountain Men, the first wave of the storied Tennessee Volunteers. The Beaty family has continued the tradition in successive generations. Alan's father, Keith, endured some of the thickest fighting in Vietnam. Alan himself did four different stints, the last as a U.S.-government-employed mercenary commanding Ugandan and Bosnian security forces. Like their ancestor, bitten by a rattlesnake during the final assault on the British loyalists at Kings Mountain, none of the Beatys returned home from their service unscathed. Alan's wife is gone. He has no hearing in one ear, a constant ringing. Veterans Affairs gave him one of those sound-effects radios to help him sleep— and also a ton of prescription pills. The ghosts of his past are constantly aswirl. They come to him in dreams, they come to him awake: Staff Sergeant Anthony Goodwin, beloved platoon leader, a Marine's Marine—shot in the face and killed instantly; Staff Sergeant Kendall Ivy, Goodwin's battlefield replacement—killed two days later, he remembers, by a small piece of shrapnel that entered just below his ass cheek and nicked an artery, causing him to bleed out; the men in Ivy's AAV, a large armored troop carrier with tank-like tracks— burned to a crisp, their bodies had to be peeled from the wreckage.

Beaty and Ivy were good friends. After a mission, they'd hang in Beaty's can at Al Asad air base in western Iraq and have a shot or two of whiskey—regular shipments from Beaty's dad came masquerading as Listerine mouthwash. Ivy's wife was pregnant. The night before he was killed, he and Beaty were watching a DVD of The Alamo, starring Billy Bob Thornton, talking all kinds of shit about going back in a time machine to kick some Mexican ass—*Gotta get us a coonskin cap!* They were U.S. Marines. Brothers in combat. Men trained to hunger for a fight, even as they were recovering from the last, even as they dreaded the next. Now Beaty keeps Ivy's shot glass in a cabinet in his dining room. One thing that wasn't lost.

After Goodwin, after Ivy, the operational leadership of the 2nd Marine Expeditionary Force's RCT-2 Jump Platoon—a bodyguarding element assigned to an impossibly tall and fearless colonel whose mission was to pacify the largely Sunni western Iraq province of Al

Anbar—had fallen to Sergeant Alan Beaty, thirty-one.

Upon receipt of his promotion, at the cost of his best friend's life, Beaty retreated to his can, which is what they call the pre-fab barracks. He put his face in his hands and cried like a little boy. *If there's anything you can do to take me out of this, Lord, please do it now. I don't want the responsibility of these Marines on my hands.*

That was 2005, more than six years—and two more deployments—ago. He still can't drive past a dead dog or a bag of garbage lying by the side of a road. The smell of burning trash. The smell of diesel fuel. The loud report of a firearm in the hollow. A rubber hose stretched across a street to count traffic. A line of slow, stupid, complaining motherfuckers at the checkout line at the Walmart... *anything* can set him off. The way people look at him. The way his family tried to treat him with kid gloves, like some cripple. The way he couldn't even bond with his own kids.

The VA awarded him 100 percent disability: post-traumatic stress disorder. Social Security told him to get a job. It's like he's home, but he's not. Like part of him was left behind. Maybe that's why he kept going back.

One year ago, Beaty rode his favorite horse eighteen miles out from his farm into the wilderness, a .40-cal pistol hanging from the pommel horn of his saddle. He was broke and depressed. He felt a little bit guilty about some of the stuff that was done overseas, and angry about other stuff. As part of a post-Blackwater crackdown on contract mercenaries, he'd been arrested and jailed on inflated charges involving an assault committed by a man under his command. The charges were finally dropped; thankfully, his dad had borne the financial burden of his defense. Home again on U.S. soil, faced with building a life... well, he didn't know who he was. He'd felt useless and unproductive and off, you know? Just off. Like nothing was ever quite right. And so goddam tired. What he would do for some sleep.

He was FUBAR, as they say in the Corps.

Fucked-Up Beyond All Repair.

He just couldn't handle it no more.

He planned carefully. Thought it through. It became kind of

an obsession, getting all the details slotted. Something to keep him busy, to keep him slogging forward, one foot in front of the other. He considered slitting his wrists in the bathtub, taking an overdose of his prescription drugs. He decided he didn't want anybody he knew to find him dead.

At last he settled on Leonides—half-Arabian, half saddlebred. Leo knows his way all over the mountain. He is famously ground tied—you can drop the reins and he'll stand for six hours in one place till you get back. Alan had figured Leo would stand over his body awhile, wondering in his loyal equine pea brain what to do next. But eventually he'd get hungry and come back to the barn. They'd send out a search party. Let the professionals deal with such things...

***

Now, driving the Honda along the rutted road, Beaty worries his goatee. Up before dawn, he is nearing the end of a six-hour round-trip drive to the Nashville airport. Of course, he would have driven six days. *One of my Marines is in trouble.* He glances to his right, checking the welfare of his passenger. His name is Pat Myers. As far as Beaty is concerned, what happened to Myers is on him.

I was extremely uncomfortable with the new platoon sergeant who was succeeding me. He wasn't the guy for the job. He was scared to go outside the wire. He didn't know how to run a convoy. He'd never get in a lead vehicle, because that's the one that always got hit. He didn't know how to do any of that crap, and he didn't want to learn.

And then I leave him alone for twelve hours, not even that, and he's done wounded three of my Marines.

Beaty spotted Myers right away at the farthest bay of the baggage claim. He saw the wheelchair, recognized the tattoo on the back of his right arm, a big cross that covers his whole triceps. They served together for nearly a year, ran eighty-four documented mobile combat patrols, always in vehicle two of the convoy. Beaty rode in the passenger seat. Lance Corporal Pat Myers sat right behind. Though he was rated as a radio operator, Myers never once touched the comms—instead, he carried a 12-gauge shotgun, the door breacher. Myers was known in the platoon as the guy who could always make everyone laugh with his irreverent humor. No matter how dark things got, he always had some smart-ass quip to lighten the mood. He saved Beaty's ass on Route Uranium, between the city of Hit and Al Asad, when he noticed their Humvee was parked directly on top of a thin green wire connected to three 120mm rockets buried in the sand. Seeing his tattoo across the airport concourse, it occurred to Beaty how many times he had followed that cross straight into the asshole of the unknown.

The last time Beaty had seen Myers was five years earlier, on the Marine Corps birthday, November 10, 2005. Elsewhere in the world, Marines in Dress Blues were attending formal balls to honor their beloved branch. Lance Corporal Myers, twenty-two, was mounting up for patrol, his first in nearly two months.

For all his joking around, Myers was clearly a troubled kid. His father had been career Army, medical discharge. His mother was a nurse. The family moved around a lot—Indiana, Alaska, Texas. "My dad was an ass," Myers would later say. "He just expected way too much of me. When I was a teenager, I went to church. I played nearly every sport. I was even in band. He never came to one concert, one game, nothing. He was one of those guys, no matter how hard I tried to please him it was never enough. I could never get it right with him. I always made these standards for myself, and they never, ever met his."

Three years after high school, Myers was working in a grocery store. He met a local recruiter. "My dad told me I wasn't man enough to be a Marine," Myers recalled. "That's the main reason I joined."

Natural athlete that he was, Myers flew through basic training and the School of Infantry. Eventually he was assigned to the jump platoon. He thought he'd found his place. Until he encountered an unexpected complication: He fell in love with a female Marine.

Beaty had seen this kind of thing before. He preached to the kid; of course he wouldn't listen—never mind that now. Everyone who has ever been around Marines knows this: They do love the same way they do war. They went on a $7,000 cruise together. After two seemingly blissful weeks, on the gangplank exiting, she told him she'd found somebody else.

When he returned to Al Asad, Myers was a train wreck. He'd come over to Beaty's can and cry—Beaty actually gave him two weeks off to get his shit together, unofficial time away from duty. During this time, Myers didn't shave, didn't shower, didn't do shit but mope around and act demented. One day, he was walking across the base wearing civvies, sporting a full beard. As it happened, he passed Colonel Stephen W. Davis, the regimental commander he was being paid by the Marine Corps to protect.

Colonel Davis did a double take. "Are you okay, Myers?"

"What's up?" Myers called. He issued a goofy wave and kept on strolling.

Within three minutes, Beaty's radio was blowing up. The sergeant major chewed his ass. Myers was pulled from the jump, given gate guard duty—six hours on, six hours off.

Six long weeks. Whenever the jump convoy would return from a mission, Myers would be waving them into the gate. *And us throwing bottles at him and stuff. Giving him a ton of shit. Ha ha, look at you, gate guard.*

Finally, Myers could take no more. He begged with tears in his eyes, "Please let me get back on the jump."

Beaty talked to the sergeant major, went to the mat for the kid. Myers got the thumbs-up.

There was only one problem: Beaty wouldn't be there to supervise. His deployment was over. He was one wake-up from going home.

Myers reported for duty the next morning. He'd shaved... everything except his moustache. Of course, the sergeant major went batshit. *As soon as we get back, you're gonna shave your fuckin' face, Marine!*

Then the new platoon sergeant informed Myers that someone else now carried the 12-gauge. Myers would be driving vehicle five, the caboose. He'd driven only once before. That time, his Humvee was hit by a roadside bomb; he'd narrowly escaped death; he'd vowed never to drive again.

Not that anybody gave two shits what he'd vowed.

All he remembers is a huge explosion. It was like the ground came up to meet him; then everything went black.

He woke up clear of the wreckage. He knew he was fucked: The tough-as-nails sergeant major was holding his hand like somebody's mommy. "I guess this means I don't have to shave," Myers said, and everybody laughed.

In the Nashville airport, what was left of Lance Corporal Pat Myers pivoted his chair to face Beaty, each hand working a wheel in opposition.

Beaty couldn't believe what he was seeing. Both of Myers' legs were gone above the knee, a couple of fingers were missing. He was heavier then Beaty remembered; his jug-eared face wore signs of successive generations of fights. He looked like shit, really, like he just didn't care no more, didn't have nothing in the world to look forward to. The other night in Ft. Worth, he'd gotten so fucked-up he'd left his wheelchair in the parking lot of a roadhouse. He'd driven home fine, but then he had to crawl up the driveway to his house.

The next morning, after a call from a concerned friend, a Marine gunnery sergeant, assigned his case by the Corps' Wounded Warriors Regiment, let herself into Myers' house with a key he'd given her for these kinds of occasions, which were becoming too numerous to count. Myers was already facing a DUI. He seemed to have hit rock bottom.

After rousing him the best she could, Gunny Teresa Grandinetti pulled out her cell phone and dialed a number. She handed it to Myers.

"Who is this?" Myers demanded insolently.

The Tennessee twang was unmistakable: "This is Sergeant Beaty."

Myers got real quiet. "Sarge, I'm really fucked-up." He burst into tears.

"You wanna come out here and stay with me a while?"

"Can I come tonight?"

As it happened, Gunny Grandinetti's husband is an employee

of Southwest Airlines; he finagled Myers a free ticket. They had him on a plane the next day.

***

The GPS signal cuts out about a mile from the house, at the clearing by an antique whitewashed church where the congregants are said to handle snakes. The cell phone dies a few hundred yards later—the Honda is picked up instead by a pack of abandoned dogs Beaty has adopted, barking and yipping and running alongside like a welcoming committee. (His old blind dog waits behind. You can kick a deflated soccer ball anywhere in the field and he'll find it and bring it back... eventually.)

As Beaty pulls up in the gravel before his modest cracker-box house, he fights a twinge of doubt. *Holy shit,* he tells himself, *now we got another mouth to feed.* And then he tells himself: *Who knows where he'd have ended up if I didn't come get him.*

Maybe like Keith Hull, living under a bridge before he came to crash with Beaty. Or Jason Delong. He was in the turret of a truck when they hit a double-stacked antitank mine; he flew in from California just to spend two days at the farm, 260 acres of cleared fields and forest and untended walnut trees deep in a hollow near Oneida, Tennessee, a hamlet of 3,800 in the far north central part of the state, just across the border from Kentucky. Or Adam Hand, another turret gunner, living hand-to-mouth in Washington, D.C. He stayed for a few weeks. Now he's a mall cop; he's thinking of coming back down. Or Spencer Pellecer, still on active duty at the School of Infantry at Camp Lejeune, who finds his way every holiday to Beaty's copious and embracing leather couch—Pellecer's mother calls Beaty for updates on her own son. Or the score of other Marines who have found work, camaraderie and refuge at Beaty's farm since June of 2008, a sort of do-it-yourself halfway house for Marines broken by war. Some stay for a week; some stay for months; one guy is working on year number two. Though Beaty has been asked informally by the Marines to help out from time to time, he has up to now gotten no formal support or guidance from them or the government; lately he's been thinking about applying for grants, soliciting contributions—something to help make his idea more serviceable than the sets of bunk beds in his kids' room. For now, it's a jerry-rigged operation. Whatever it takes, they make it work.

If only there were room for all of them.

Horses graze in the field behind the house; mountains rise in the middle distance. A small rickety porch with three steps frames the doorway. Off to one side is a pile of fresh lumber, two-bys and four-bys and such.

The engine hiccups to a stop. "Look Devil Dog, I ain't lifting your fat ass up into the house," Beaty says, a tone of command once again swelling the barrel of his chest. He gestures toward the lumber pile. "You're gonna have to build your own ramp."

Hungover, fucked-up, possibly suicidal, Myers stares at his former platoon leader. It is hot as hell, the sun was beating down, fat bees were buzzing everywhere. He is twenty-five years old. He's been blown up and bled out. His lungs collapsed, his heart stopped three times. When he finally awoke from his medically induced coma, he found himself in a hospital in Washington, D.C. The first person he saw was his mother. *I asked her if my junk was still there.* After that, he spent two years in an army hospital in San Antonio.

Beaty climbs out of the truck and shuts his door, heading for the house. "When you get the ramp built," he tells Myers, "you can roll yourself inside, and I'll pour you a drink of whiskey, and we'll talk about the war."

***

On a somnolent afternoon at Beaty's farm six months later, rain drums relentlessly on the tin roof overhanging the back porch; dense fog looms, obscuring the thickly forested mountains. A war flick plays at low volume on the big screen in the living room— King Leonidas is leading his elite Spartans into battle against a vastly superior force. The sounds of children's laughter and video games drift out from one of the bedrooms, Beaty's three kids in residence for the weekend.

Four men sprawl on sofas around a big, old wood-burning stove, sipping beer and moonshine. His first night in the house alone, Beaty slept on the wall-to-wall carpet by the stove, too heavy for his wife to move, he supposes. Now, there's a hardwood floor. After he built the ramp, Myers put in the floor. (Of course, Beaty worked by his side... as he'd ended up doing with the ramp.)

Myers has been gone four months. He's back in Fort Worth, has a girlfriend and a baby; he and a partner are working on a plan to train vets as mechanics. He still visits from time to time—you should have seen him driving the hay wagon with broom handles duct-taped to his stumps so he could work the pedals. Later they duct-taped him onto a smooth-gaited Tennessee walking horse and took him for a ride up the mountain. Obviously, his time with Beaty, and the camaraderie of the Marines who are always coming and going from the place, helped turn him around. The truth is, you come home, and nobody understands. While you've been out killing and trying to survive, they've been shopping for groceries, ordering wine in fancy restaurants, attending to math homework. (It helped also that Gunny Grandinetti finally got the military to send Myers a pair of prosthetic legs.)

More recently, Myers' room at the farm has been occupied by Keith Hull. Skeleton-thin with dreadlocks, the former sergeant is wearing his usual surfer shorts and rubber flip-flops despite the cold. Hull was raised in private schools, the rebellious son of a successful insurance man. He tried high-rise steel construction before joining the Corps in 1998. Following 9/11, he was assigned to Task Force 58, the first Marines on the deck in Afghanistan; they pushed straight through to Kandahar. After mustering out, Hull attempted college for several years. When he was recalled by the Marines in 2004, he was assigned to Beaty's jump platoon as a turret gunner. "The best platoon the Marine Corps has ever made up," he says.

"Everybody was experienced," Hull remembers. "Everybody had a different MOS. It was like a James Bond platoon: No matter what situation we were in—say there was a tank to be moved, or a piece of equipment that needed to be fixed, what have you—there was always somebody who knew how." Out of twenty-three in the platoon during his deployment, two were killed, four wounded. The psychic toll is yet untallied. Several months after his return, the sergeant who replaced Beaty was thrown from his motorcycle after driving off a road. There were a lot of rumors about a suicide note in his back pocket. Only the family knows for sure.

According to a recent federal appeals court ruling that took the VA to task for failing to care for veterans suffering from PTSD, an average of eighteen vets (from all eras) commit suicide every day.

Of 1.6 million Iraq/Afghan war vets, according to a 2008 Rand Corporation study cited by the U.S. 9th Circuit Court of Appeals, 300,000 suffer from PTSD or major depression. As of 2011, the number of vets from those wars surpassed 2 million.

By the time Hull came to Beaty's farm, he'd spiraled into homelessness. A proud and intelligent man with a gift for cleverly bending a truth, he'll tell you he was "stealth camping" while working as a bar bouncer, getting paid off the books in drugs and alcohol. That he ended up sleeping under bridges, he explains, was inspired by a Web site he came across. Admittedly, he was a sorry case. His apartment was gone; he'd donated all his furniture to needy neighbors. His girlfriend was gone and so was most of the contents of his bank account. (He'd have given her the money if she'd only asked.) He'd lost his job as a janitor in a small restaurant— he worked the night shift because he couldn't stand to be around so many people; a can of beans would fall off a shelf, and he'd dive for cover. He was drunk or high all the time. He'd gotten to the point where he'd asked his father to lock up his guns. "I was ready to go the way of the dodo," he says.

Now Hull is chillin' in Beaty's living room, where he's pretty much been part of the furniture for the last nine months. At the moment, he's helping to play host to the dignitary who's just come limping up the new front ramp. (At least he's not in the bedroom staring at the popcorn ceiling. In the beginning, that's all he did. It was Beaty who finally dragged him to the VA to start him on treatment.)

Lieutenant Colonel Tim Maxwell, forty-six, is one of the highest-ranking Marines to be seriously wounded in Iraq. While in the hospital recovering from traumatic brain and other injuries sustained on his sixth overseas tour, he began ministering to wounded Devil Dogs, going from bed to bed in his bathrobe. Eventually he saw to fruition his dream of creating a Wounded Warriors Regiment, a unit to keep account of Marines after they'd been injured—a series of barracks and facilities and social services where the wounded can begin their recovery in the embrace of their fellows. The first such barracks, at Camp Lejeune in North Carolina, was named in his honor.

Like many wounded vets, Maxwell has discovered that what's broken can never really be fixed. There are ongoing complications, constant tinkerings with meds, weird side effects, oddly unexplainable medical breakdowns, revisionary surgeries. In 2008, Maxwell had an operation to remove the remaining shrapnel from his brain—originally the doctors thought it was embedded too deep to risk extracting. As it turned out, the toxins leaching from the metal were cooking his noodle—*How do you like that?* He had reached the point where he was losing more function every day.

The surgery, following a long and tortured rehab, eased some of Maxwell's speech, behavioral, and cognitive problems. But it also left the strapping former triathlete without use of his right arm, with tenuous balance, and with a greatly reduced field of vision on his right side. More recently he needed further surgery on his rebuilt left elbow—all the metal had attracted a horrendous infection. "The doc wanted to put me in a cast for six weeks. I said, 'You're talking about me having to have somebody wipe my butt again. I'm not okay with that,'" Maxwell will later recall over dinner, having opted for lasagna at the best steakhouse in Oneida, because he couldn't cut the meat with one hand, and because he was too proud to let somebody do it for him.

A few months ago, Maxwell flew from his home in northern Virginia to the Marine base at Camp Pendleton, north of San Diego to try out for a Wounded Warriors Paralympics team. Despite his balance problems, he managed to ride his bike one-armed for eighteen miles without crashing. Swimming proved more difficult. Sank like a stone. A guy he met wants to teach him how to swim with one arm. Maxwell doesn't want to learn. Neither does he want to learn to write with his left hand. He is convinced he can rehab the damn right limb if he just keeps working. Already he can make his fingers move a little.

Having heard a lot of talk about Beaty's farm, Maxwell has driven his specially equipped camper van (license plate BUMR) nearly 600 miles from Camp Lejeune, where he was attending the dedication of a brand-new Wounded Warriors barracks. After Maxwell founded the first barracks in 2007, an entire Wounded Warrior Regiment was formed. There's a command center at Quantico, Virginia, now a second barracks at Camp Pendleton, and satellite offices around the country. Since its inception, Maxwell's regiment has helped nearly 27,000 wounded Marines. But the program benefits primarily Marines still on active duty. For those who have left the service, help is hard to find.

Retired now from the Corps, Maxwell runs SemperMax.Com, a nonprofit support group for wounded Marines, both active and vets. He has a Web site and a zillion contacts. (As does his wife, Shannon, also active in helping wounded families. She has recently authored a children's book, *Our Daddy is Invincible!*, aimed at helping kids cope when their parents suffer injuries at war.) Each day brings Maxwell a different project, a different hard-luck tale, another wounded Marine with a problem to solve—which means that each day Maxwell has something important to do. He would have arrived at Beaty's place sooner, but he couldn't drive straight through; he doesn't see very well in the dark anymore, either.

Of course, he drove some distance in the dark anyway.

"After six and a half years, the doctors are starting to tell me they don't know what to do for me," Maxwell is telling the others. Though his speech is slurred and he likes to play himself off as a humble, brain-damaged crip, Maxwell's mind is sharp, his ideas run well before the wind, his gruff irreverence is intact. "Doctors never say 'I don't know.' Those three words: They're frickin' *restricted* from saying that."

"They might lose their status as gods," Hull quips.

"The most irritating thing to me is the doctors grouping PTSD and traumatic brain injuries together because they know so little about the damn brain. They're saying we got the same problems, me and you. Well, hello? Our problems are *totally* different. They both suck. But they suck different. Like with my injury, my brain is wacked. Shrapnel is what got me, not the *kaboom*."

"There's an actual physical injury," Beaty says.

"Exactly," says Hull.

"I know I'm supposed to be a dumbass grunt, but even I can tell the difference between who's got what," Maxwell says. Though he was born in Ohio, he has a Southern accent that showed up after the initial injury, the result of an enemy mortar round that landed serendipitously within the sandbagged doorway of his tent inside a command base. "When I was in the Wounded Warriors barracks, you'd see the PTSD guys up talking to each other at 2:00 a.m. None of them could sleep. What about you?"

Hull shrugs. *Who gives a shit.*

"You're kind of new at it—you have to learn how to fight the fight," Maxwell says.

"That's the thing that's so jacked up about PTSD," Hull says. "It's a mental degradation that you can't describe. If you hurt your arm, you have a mark. But if you hurt your mind... it's like, *Whatthefuck,* you know? I'm like, *I've been through some bad shit before, much worse shit than this. Why can't I fix myself now?*"

"I think everybody who goes through combat has PTSD," Maxwell says.

"The experts say it's like 20 percent," Beaty offers.

Maxwell screws up his face like he's smelled something bad. "That's 'cause when you go to treatment, they ask the wrong questions. The first thing they should ask is: Did you experience combat? Did you have to return fire? Then they should ask: Did you ever lose a friend? 'Cause when you see a dude get wacked, a friend of yours, a stranger, it don't matter—it always fucks you up."

"What person in combat ain't lost a friend?" Hull asks.

"Exactly," says Beaty.

"You spend the rest of your life lying awake at night thinking: If I didn't do such and such, then Tommy Smith wouldn't be dead,"

Maxwell says. "It's always: my fault, my fault, my fault. I should've been on the left side of the Hummer. I should have been on the right. I should have gone first through the door. There's no way around it."

"The problem is getting guys into treatment," Beaty says. "My dad was a Marine in Vietnam. A Suicide Charlie guy. Served in 1968. Purple Heart. He's had PTSD his whole life—but he only just started to get treatment when I did. He's been gutting it out for like thirty, forty years. Bad dreams, cold sweats, the whole nine. And he never told a soul."

"It's damn embarrassing," Maxwell says. "You've got to convince a guy he's got PTSD. You gotta be like: 'Don't feel like a wuss. It's a real injury.'"

Hull: "The docs are like, 'Tell me about your issues.' But it's hard to explain. Because sometimes I don't even have words to express how it makes me feel. And the docs are like, 'Well, you gotta come up with something.' And I'm just like, *Fuck*, you know? It feels like something's trying to come out of my chest. Like in *Alien*? That's how I think of it—it feels like something is trying to rip through my chest. It's like: I don't understand it either, motherfucker! I just know I'm fucked-up and I need help. I'm just really at the point where I want to fucking get my shit together and move on."

"Are you taking your meds?"

"I take something for my rage issues—so I know that works. And then I only take my other ones when I have panic attacks. Those pills are weird. It's like they make my insides calm down, but it doesn't make my brain stop working. You know what I'm saying? It's like my brain is still going *What the fuck? What the fuck? What the fuck?*"

Maxwell takes a swig of his beer. "I have days where I just sit there and... " his voice trails off. The lamp light catches the jagged scar on the side of his head, just below the hedge line of his high-and-tight military fade.

***

Beaty and Maxwell judder back down the rutted road on the

way to town for an early dinner. Hull has volunteered to stay home with the kids, the eldest of whom is now fifteen. The sky has cleared, and the moon has risen, presiding over the twilight and bare trees. With the windows down, you can hear the water in Stanley Creek, more of a rush than a babble.

Beaty points out his barn, a circa-1960s corncrib renovated by Marines, and his locust fence posts—harvested, hauled down the mountain, and set in place by Marines. "And see right here on the left? Keith Hull cleared that entire field. It was nothing but woods when he started. He disked it up and sowed it and did everything by himself." Most of the fields were cleared by Marines.

"It's not me asking them to come work," Beaty tells the retired colonel. "That's the funny thing. They just show up because they want a place to go." He shakes his head, the way a person does when he feels both blessed and perplexed. "Sometimes it gets a little bit crowded."

"I'm sure there's plenty of work to be done," Maxwell says.

"There's camaraderie," Beaty says. "There's people here that understand 'em, other combat Marines. We sit around at night, and I'm not gonna lie, we sit around and have a drink or three and talk about the war. It's huge for them. This is their home."

"It's hard to feel comfortable anywhere else," Maxwell says.

Beaty scratches his head, resets his trucker cap. "When they teach you to be a Marine, they teach you to focus, because you can't be emotional in combat. You learn to be able to put things out of your mind. You learn to build walls. We've been trained to just keep functioning, to operate without emotion, without conscience. That's what you need in war.

"But once you get back to society," Beaty continues, "the walls are still up. It's hard to have an emotional attachment to people. Because in your mind, you've been trained to know that this right here could be your last day on earth. So why allow myself to be connected to this woman? Why allow myself to be connected to my children? Lucky I got an amazing woman therapist now at the VA. It's only in the last few months that I'm learning how to take the walls down."

"The main strength of the Marine Corps is also the main weakness," Maxwell says matter-of-factly. "We're *too* well trained."

"They make 'em Marines, but nobody ever turns them back into civilians," Beaty says. "Even prisoners get halfway houses. Druggies get sober living."

Maxwell looks out the window. Crisscrossing the country, he's heard it all a million times before. He grinds his jaw, the wheels turn.

"Let's just estimate," Maxwell says at last. "What if we got a hundred grand? You'd be amazed with what we could do in this place with 100k. We make a campsite. When each kid comes in, we give him some lumber and we let him build his own cabin. We could have ten, twelve cabins, a rec hall—"

"I could sure put 'em to work," Beaty says. "Right now, the only thing we're taking off the farm is hay. I thought about turning it into a tomato farm. And I got enough walnut trees to fill fifteen dump trucks with walnuts. But it's too labor-intensive. Right now, I just have to let shit rot."

"It's like that movie. With that actor, you know? He builds the whatchacallit behind his—" Maxwell knits his brow, searching for the proper noun. People, places, things. It's called aphasia. It's part of the brain injury; there's no escaping it.

"*Field of Dreams?*" Beaty offers gingerly.

"If you build it, they will come," Maxwell says, pleased to remember the damn quote.

Yes! Yes! Yes! Beaty is thinking.

Turning his farm into a heaven for Marines—it's one of the reasons he decided to ride his horse back down the mountain that fateful day.

***

Seventy miles south of Alan Beaty's farm, John Cybula is sitting at a picnic table on the back deck of a house belonging to his girlfriend's mom. His stealth-black, Hi-Point 9mm semiautomatic pistol is broken down on the table; we've just finished emptying a few mags of hollow points into an assortment of car-stereo amps and tree stumps and other unfortunate objects that live for that purpose in the backyard. In a little while he'll demonstrate how fast he can put it back together with his eyes shut. Like he says, "Gotta stay sharp."

Cybula is twenty-five. He brings to mind Elvis Presley in his thirties, a handsome devil gone a little bit puffy, a certain darkness around the eyes, his hair carefully gelled and spiked. Chelsea is by his side; they share a pack of cigs. She is twenty-one, sweet as can be, taking the semester off from community college—she's thinking either forestry or nursing. She's got blue eyes and a trim little bod, an asymmetrical haircut with a pink swath dyed into the back, about as fashionista as it gets around Madisonville, Tennessee, a town so small that you can be shopping for a toothbrush at 2:00 a.m. at the local Walmart and be spotted by the local cop, who is aware that you are wanted for a probation violation. (He let Cybula kiss his girl goodnight and took him to jail without cuffs.)

Cybula followed his granddad into the Marine Corps at seventeen, another boy from another family of Tennessee Volunteers—a high school quarterback who majored in cheerleaders, who wanted payback for 9/11. When we first met, in the summer of 2007, he was twenty-one. He'd been wounded in Fallujah, caught a bullet in the hip. The impact knocked him off a roof; he fell three stories and broke his pelvis. Young and gung-ho, not wanting to be the weak link in the chain, he tried to rejoin his unit before the bones had properly healed. He ended up at the Wounded Warriors barracks at Camp Lejeune, eating a fistful of meds every day.

The sky is blue, the sun is unseasonably warm, a dog sleeps at his feet. "When I first got out, I was really lost," Cybula says. "I didn't know what to do. I was on all those pain meds. It hurt to stand or sit or lie down. The only thing I was trained to do since I was seventeen was how to kill somebody. But it's not really a marketable skill. It kind of works against you, even.

"Like, I got in a fight with my stepdad. He came at me with a baseball bat. He swung, and I caught it, and I jerked it away from him. And you should have seen the look in his face. He knew he'd done the wrong thing. I just destroyed him. He had some messed-up vertebras in his neck. I broke his jaw, his eye socket, a couple of his ribs.

"When the police came, I explained it to them—he came at me with a baseball bat, you know? Self-defense. But they arrested me for aggravated assault, assault with a deadly weapon, because of my Marine Corps training.

"After that I started abusing drugs bad again—I ain't going to lie to you, I started shooting up OxyContin and crap like that. I was on drugs so bad like I had to pawn my TV, my car, everything I had. It's just like, I don't know. I went to war, I did this, I did that. I have lots of feelings inside my head; I try to tuck them away—but they always come out. I don't know how to deal with these feelings. You can ask her: Sometimes I'll just flip out and like our dog will do the littlest thing and like, what was it? What did Roxy-dog do that one night where I was wanting to take her out back and like just like blow her head off?"

Chelsea: "I don't remember what she did."

"She did something to me and I was just so pissed that I was like—"

"The one thing we fight about is the dogs," Chelsea says, "There's a difference between discipline and beating them, you know?"

"I don't like hurting her," Cybula says. He looks down the barrel of his weapon, making sure the chamber is clean. "I'm going to the VA now. They put me on Xanax so I'm more chill."

"He still has the worst dreams," Chelsea says.

"Tell him about the time you got up without telling me. Remember I grabbed you?"

"He sometimes just starts crying. And like, at first, I didn't want to wake him up, you know? I was afraid or whatever. So I finally asked him, I was like, 'If you have a bad dream, do you want me to wake you up?' And he was like, 'I feel like such a pussy for crying.'"

"And then I've also sleepwalked," Cybula says. "Like I woke up in my boxers standing out in the woods here behind the house. And I was like, *What am I doing outside?* It was crazy. Sometimes I can be so happy. Like, alive? And then all of the sudden I'll just be like, my head is down. And she'll be like, 'What's wrong?' And I'll just be like, 'Nothin,' and then I'll cry or something. And then sometimes I'll just be really, really *mad*. And she'll go, 'What's wrong, honey?' And I'll just be like 'Don't talk to me.' That's why I got this pistol. Believe it or not, I don't want to hurt nobody. It's like an outlet, you know? Like when I get pissed, I'll come outside and shoot it. That's what we did in the Marine Corps. We let off steam by shooting guns and stuff like that."

Chelsea takes two cigarettes from the pack, hands one to her man. Gallantly, he lights hers first; she smiles at him adoringly. They don't know it yet, but she's pregnant.

Fifty Grand in San Diego

Shun Ducksworth lives with his wife and two kids in a duplex condo close to the beach. And not far from the edge. A look at the modern version of the American Dream—an out-of-work ex-Marine playing Mr. Mom, finding a silver cloud in a dirty diaper.

R ising with effort from the overstuffed couch, the baby secured in the crook of his mahogany python of a limb like an M16 rifle at shoulder arms, Stacey LaShun Ducksworth, thirty-two years old, lets out a bone-weary sigh.

"*Lordy, Lordy, Lordy*," he declaims, his eyes rolling heavenward, toward the rough-textured plaster ceiling of his 800-square-foot duplex condo, secured as of now with a rock-bottom, interest-only loan, due to balloon in three years, another of the myriad swords of Damocles hanging over his head. He sniffs the air in the vicinity of his daughter, Addison Leann Ducksworth, ten months old, dressed in a pink-and-white Ralph Lauren onesie, a hand-me-down from friends. His nose wrinkles; his face contorts into a mock-hideous mask.

"Let's go, Jackson," he orders the three-year-old. His voice is a deep baritone with a hint of Mississippi Delta twang—the only giveaway his tendency to drop his *th*'s in favor of *d*'s—a commanding voice, perfectly suited to a man who rose to the rank of sergeant after only four years in the Marines. With the index finger of his right hand, in which he holds Addison's bottle, her blankie, and a plastic toy bird from McDonald's, he pokes off their thirty-two-inch Zenith television, bought on special seven years ago at Costco, as was much of what they own. Did you know that Costco even has real estate agents?

"Let's go, Jackson," he repeats. With children, unlike Marines, you *always* have to issue an order more than once. "Let's go, buddy," a tad louder this time. "I need to change your sister. Are you ready for your nap? Come over here, and let me blow your nose." A decade ago, he was ducking bullets in Mogadishu.

Jackson William Ducksworth is sitting on the floor with a forty-eight-piece farmyard puzzle, just completed. He was born two weeks before his mom was supposed to start her internship at a naval hospital, a requirement for her master's degree in social work. Despite the emergency C-section, she reported ten minutes early on the scheduled day. That is her trademark; she is *always* ten minutes early. (Another trademark: proving people wrong. Like the time her father told her she would surely flunk out of college if she transferred to be closer to a man he had yet to allow inside his house.) Back in those days, during her internship, Tuesdays were the worst: work from 6:30 a.m. till 3:30 p.m., home to breast-feed Jackson, night classes, studying, bed. At the time, of course, her husband was the breadwinner, making nearly $50,000 a year as a manager of a Footlocker. His closet is still full of vintage Air Jordans. She herself owns exactly six pairs of shoes. Every time she buys a new pair, she donates an old pair. That is her personal policy. The kids do the same with their toys.

Like his mom, Jackson has asthma, which seems to open him up to every bug and flu that comes down the pike. He's been sick now for several days—most of the last several months, if you add it up. They've begun seeing a homeopathic doctor, $400 for the first consultation. They put it on the credit card, even though they vowed to use it now only for emergencies, like the $600 vet bill after their cat was attacked by a coyote, or the brand-new KitchenAid mixer—in black to match the self-timing coffeemaker—that Stacey LaShun

Duckworth bought recently as a surprise for his wife, Heather Marie Peterson Ducksworth, even though they can't afford it.

Twin rivers of viscous green snot flow from Jackson's nostrils, puddle above his lips. From the moment he awoke this morning—if you can call it *awoke*, because he never really went to sleep, he was really up all night, on and off, off and on, waking up his little sister, calling for his mommy... *Mommy... MOMMY!*... even though Mommy was immobilized with a pulled muscle in her back and needed her rest so she could go to work the next day—from the moment he woke up, asking again for Mommy, who was already gone, Jackson has been cranky and high maintenance, couldn't walk down the stairs himself, couldn't go potty himself, knocking over the orange juice that he insisted on having in a big-guy glass instead of his sippy cup, asking every minute for a tissue, literally every minute, *Blow my nose, Daddy, blow my nose, Daddy*, the word like an exclamation point, a direct order, a command from on high... Daddy... *Daddy... DAAAAAAAD-DYYYYYYYY!!!!!*... the inconsolable trill of a three-year-old, which, every parent discovers, is the true age for terrible twos.

"Jackson," he implores, as calmly as he is able, "put the puzzle back in the box, please."

"I very sick, Daddy."

"I know you are, buddy." Another sigh. "*Please.* Put the puzzle in the box. You need your nap. And I need to get some studying done. Remember? My classes?"

"Your *college* classes, Daddy."

Jackson sticks out his tongue and coughs—phlegmy, pitiful, an Oscar-caliber demonstration of the truly dire state of his health. His skin is eggshell white with a squirt of brown tint, like what they do with ceiling paint at Home Depot. He has his mom's pointy nose and prominent chin, her smallish down-turned eyes, her impish stick-out ears. His head is covered with a woolen thatch of tight yellow ringlets, which his daddy—who once did a six-month stint as the ship's barber on the USS Essex—trims painstakingly, using a comb, scissors, and electric trimmer, one little ringlet at a time.

Jackson sticks out his tongue and coughs again for effect, the tiny pink tongue of a baby doll, curled at the edges, *cough, cough,*

cough, and then again, *cough*, *cough*, and then, suddenly, he is seized by a fit of real coughing, deep rattling hacks that rack his thin and insubstantial body, touching off in turn a fountain of tears, huge crocodile tears that flow down his cheeks, mingling with the snot and the drool, splashing upon the Pergo floor that his enterprising parents installed as part of their do-it-yourself home renovation, financed by Visa, a rare and impulsive bit of live-for-today thinking that nearly ruined them.

"I... don't... like... Mommy... *working!*" Jackson shrieks, a sob set between each word, his fists balled, tears and green snot flying everywhere.

Now Addison spits out her pacifier and sputters a few times, like a chain saw trying to start up, and then she catches, and she is off, too, a full-blown cry, causing Jackson, the ever-indignant former only child, to cry even harder, the two wailing now in stereo, an ear-shattering duet of inarticulate woe...

And then, Jackson throws up on the rug.

***

Another day in the condo, part of an oldish, modest development on the outskirts of San Diego called Carefree San Carlos. Along with its 800 square feet, the Ducksworth family holds title to half of a carport. Unfortunately, due to the placement of the communal washer and dryer in their particular allotted space, they can't pull either of their vehicles ('99 Nissan Altima, '03 Honda Odyssey) inside. One load of laundry costs eight quarters. Shun does approximately twenty loads a week. Everywhere he goes, he is always scrounging for quarters. You'd be surprised how many people say no.

Post-nap, the kids are on the couch, watching Disney's *Pocahontas*—a fine example of feminine pulchritude by any standard, cartoon or otherwise, especially to a guy whose last night out with his wife, sans children, was roughly twenty-one months previous, a Saturday. They saw *Man on Fire*.

Jackson appears to be feeling a little better today, thanks possibly to the homeopathic pellets he's been taking every two hours, eighteen dollars for the tube, though if you tell him he seems better, he will look up at you with doleful brown eyes and declare: "I not better. I 'till very tick"—a little problem with consonants he will no doubt outgrow, provided he quits sucking his finger, which could lead to many complications, among them a need for orthodontia, speech therapy, even corrective surgery, another of the many worst-case scenarios rattling around inside his parents' skulls. He is sitting on the far north end of the overstuffed couch in his customary pose; his finger—the right index, which he says is chocolate flavored—in his mouth, his sippy cup of apple juice by his side, and under each arm his faithful Momos, two identical furry monkeys that go everywhere.

Baby Addison is propped at the south end of the couch, which was purchased at Macy's during the Ducksworths' more frivolous days before children, along with the matching overstuffed chair that they both hate (only the cat uses it) and an armoire to hold the television, as was the style before entertainment centers came in. Addison's lids are heavy, her pink rosebud of a mouth is working her pacifier—a continuous, juicy *suck suck suck* reminiscent of Maggie on *The Simpsons*. Her face and onesie are splotched with orange-yam and green-pea baby food, the healthy, natural kind from Trader Joe's. As often seems the case in two-child families, the male Ducksworth child resembles his mom, the female her dad, both in looks and temperament—two little copies, the sexes playfully reversed. Round-faced and big-eyed with a small, flat nose, and twin topknots of fine chestnut hair, Addison puts you in mind of a darling baby bear cub—clearly her papa bear's child, though much lighter in complexion, the same eggshell white with brown tint as her brother. (Family joke: Heather's white genes are very dominant.)

At the moment, Stacey LaShun Ducksworth is sitting cross-legged on the floor, trying his best to gift-wrap a largish cardboard box, his thick fingers struggling with the intricacies. For long stretches of time, he stops what he's doing and stares upward, lost in *Pocahontas*. Back in Soso, Mississippi, population 382—where he went to church three times a week with people who spoke in tongues, where he ran the hundred-yard dash in ten-something, and where he was the first black guy ever to be elected Mr. West Jones High School, quite the Romeo despite the fact that his parents wouldn't let him go to dances or movies—everyone called him Stacey. It was only after he got to boot camp at Parris Island (where no one bothered to advise him of the long-term benefits of surrendering $1,200 of his pay in order to qualify for college-tuition benefits under the GI Bill) that he started going by the name Shun. It's supposed to be pronounced the same way as the word meaning "to avoid someone deliberately." Most people, however, pronounce it *Shawn*. He never corrects them. It's as if he's not quite committed to that name, either.

Years ago, when he was still in high school, he asked his mom, Ora Lee Ulmer Ducksworth, how come she named him Stacey. The prettiest of three girls (and seven boys) born to a sharecropper and his wife, Ora Lee was a stern disciplinarian, taken sometimes to using a tree switch, a hairbrush, or a piece of model-racing-car track to emphasize a point with her two sons, Stacey and Jermaine. Shun's father, Norman Ducksworth, no middle name, is the son of S.L. Ducksworth, who was also a sharecropper. No one ever knew what that S.L. stood for. S.L. himself said it didn't stand for nothin'. Shun sometimes wonders: Maybe it stood for Stacey. Shun's dad was a short-distance truck driver; for many years, he delivered chicken feed. He brought home a good enough living to move his family, after the second was born, from their double-wide trailer to a proper brick house on a street inhabited mostly by white people. They still live there today, hard by Big Creek, across the main highway from a little community called Cracker's Neck.

So why did his mom name him Stacey?

"Saw it in a book and liked it," explained Ora Lee in her husky, molasses-slow monotone, the prettiest girl in Soso in her day, perhaps, and still a looker at fifty-three, but never a woman of many words. The name LaShun came from his girl cousin LaShunda. Their family is close: two sisters and a brother who married two brothers and a sister. Twenty-two aunts and uncles in all; uncounted cousins.

Within that cardboard box that Shun is wrapping is a KitchenAid Artisan Series five-quart mixer. His wife, Heather, is one of those women who bakes. A lot. *A lot.* And *goo-ood*, as they like to say in Soso: two syllables, musical, emphatic, like in church. Sugar cookies. Peanut-butter cookies. Chocolate-chip cookies that Shun swears put Famous Amos to shame. Maybe too *goo-ood*, Heather jokes: Over the course of the last four years, she has been as large as a size sixteen, though she's presently down to a twelve. Ironically, in the months leading up to her first pregnancy, she was down to her smallest ever, size eight. She knows a lot of women like that. They lose all their weight, they're looking the best of their lives, the rose in full bloom. And then, bingo, they're pregnant. They never see their waistlines again. Compared with some of the women she knows, Heather looks pretty small.

Anyway, Heather's a great baker. It's something she and Jackson do together; Shun and Addison do their part by eating whatever is baked. While Jackson is a problem eater (and a problem pooper, truth be told), Addison, like her daddy, never turns down a morsel of food. Previously, Heather always used this eight-year-old Proctor Silex hand mixer she'd taken from her mom, MaryAnne Burroughs Peterson, who is sixteen years sober and smokes her fair share of cigarettes but doesn't do much baking. Two months ago, in mid-batch, the old mixer blew. There haven't been any homemade cookies since.

In a way, buying this mixer for Heather—the gesture itself, the thought behind it—is a perfect metaphor for Shun. As the saying goes, it's what you *do* that counts. Heather and Shun met eleven years ago on a fix up. He was stationed at Camp Pendleton. His Marine buddy, a white guy, knew of a busload of high school chicks from Rio Vista, California—a farm town in the central valley north of Oakland—who were coming south to San Diego for spring break.

The first time they met, first impression, Heather had no interest in Shun, who at that point was going by the nickname Duck. Part of the reason was his race, though she was by far the most liberal of her friends, the only one who ever hung out with Mexicans, which she did a little too much for her mother's taste, tooling around at all hours in her VW Beetle, primer gray with mismatched front fenders, chugging Zima and smoking Newports.

Let loose upon Pacific Beach in San Diego, the spring-break revelers, with their detachment of Marines, slogged from bar to bar, re-enacting their own version of an MTV reality show. Because she was eighteen and away from home, Heather got a tattoo, a small crescent moon at her bikini line. As the night wore on, this guy Duck—with his sweet smile and courtly manner, his chiseled shoulders and rock-hard biceps—began to look more and more attractive.

When they got back to the motel room, Heather recalls, "People were passed out all over the place, and I'm trying to sleep with Shun, and he's, you know, rejecting everything I'm trying. He's saying, like, 'No, you're too drunk. We'll do it another time.' And I'm like... in shock. That never happened with guys at home. So we go to sleep and we wake up and he's still there, which was, like, another shock, and I was like, 'I didn't think you'd stay.' And then we all went to Disneyland, and he came, too. We took the bus, and he drove in a car. The whole way, my friends, they all kept saying, like, 'Oh, he's just a one-night fling.' But I was like, 'No, I think I really like him.'"

Upon returning home, Heather told her parents, "I'm in love with a black guy," adding, "I know he'll make a great father." Her own father, Bob Peterson, a descendent of Okies, sells poisons and pesticides to farmers for a living. Sitting in the smoke-filled living room of his ranch house, Bob Peterson looked like he didn't know whether to shit or vomit or do both at the same time, as Heather recalls it. The following Christmas, Shun made his first trip to Rio Vista. He stayed at Heather's friend's place; Heather brought him back a plate of food. Nowadays, everyone gets along just fine. Shun has never begrudged Heather's dad his initial feelings. "Some people just need time," he says.

What Heather needs, Shun has decided, is a mixer. More specifically, a KitchenAid Artisan Series five-quart mixer. She's spoken of it many times. Price: $300.

There is just one little problem.

Ducksworth regular monthly expenses, including mortgage, utilities, homeowners' fees, gas, insurance and other auto expenses, health insurance for the kids, credit-card minimum payments, preschool tuition, cell phones, Costco, Trader Joe's, regular groceries: $3,298.

Special expenses (projected, upcoming), like extra food for Shun's parents' visit, road trip to Rio Vista, gifts, clothes, personal items: $700.

Amount of money Heather has taken home in four weeks as a part-time, substitute social worker at two different area hospitals: $3,800.

Amount of money in the Ducksworths' savings account: $30.

Seven months ago, the impossible happened: Stacey LaShun Ducksworth, Mr. West Jones High, was fired from his job. He'd worked for Footlocker for seven and a half years—almost ten if you include the years during high school. Though his store was the fifth-highest producer in the San Diego area, his superiors took issue with Shun's work on several counts, some of which he could have controlled (recruiting more people into the Footlocker management system, keeping more up-to-date with paperwork, cracking the whip harder on employees) and some of which he could not have controlled (the lack of square footage at his store, leaving no room for inventory, which continued nevertheless to arrive in daily shipments from two different sources, piling up everywhere, causing Shun to feel very much like Mickey in *Fantasia*, fighting a flood tide of bewitched and overpriced athletic shoes).

With the job, of course, went the health care. Also into the latrine went the deal for the new house. They'd been days from closing: three bedrooms, two baths, a washer and dryer, a yard... They'd searched for more than a year. Luckily, they were able to persuade the buyer of *their* condo to shut down the deal, which was also about to close. At first, the guy threatened to sue.

Selling price of an 1,800-square-foot duplex condo, two bedrooms, one bath, some renovation, twenty-five minutes from the Pacific Ocean: $323,000.

Within days of Shun's dismissal, Heather had him on unemployment. Though he'd sobbed via cell phone on the day of his firing, by the time he got to the condo he was dry-eyed, and he has remained so ever since. For the next six months, he received a check for $781 every two weeks. Meanwhile, Heather increased her part-time hours at a clinic run by a pair of married chiropractors; she did the books and also babysat their son. The Ducksworths also refinanced their condo, folding in all their debts (car and motorcycle payments and $20,000 on three credit cards), lowering their monthly nut considerably.

After looking for work with disappointing results, Shun realized that he was never going to find the kind of high-paying job he needed if he didn't have a college diploma. In Shun and Heather's estimation, you need at least $100,000 a year to live comfortably in California. To command that much, you need a sheepskin—or preferably, in today's America, two people with sheepskins. Their course was clear: Heather would go to work full-time; Shun would take care of the kids and go to college at night.

Now, for the first time since sixth grade—when he started his first job, at one of the chicken houses his dad delivered to—Shun is unemployed. More to the point, he is a kept man, dependent upon a woman for his very subsistence. "I feel like I'm the female," Shun says in his deep baritone. "It's like, Can I go buy this? Can I go do that and stuff? I asked her, 'Am I gonna get an allowance or anything like that?'"

Heather looked at him like he was crazy. Wives know how it works. Back when he was making the money, working fifty-five or sixty-five hours a week, Heather never thought twice about buying a new duvet cover at Bed, Bath & Beyond—provided, of course, that it was on sale. "Both our names are on the checking account," she told him. "It's your money, too."

And so it was that Shun decided that he was going to buy Heather a KitchenAid Artisan Series five-quart mixer, the kind she'd always talked about, the kind she really wanted, the kind she would never have bought for herself. Though he didn't say it out loud, and though he didn't even think about it this way until he was asked—

like his mother, whom he resembles, Shun is not a man of many words—the reason he really wanted to buy the mixer for Heather wasn't just that he was hungry for some of her chocolate-chip cookies. It was just, well... he wanted to let her know how much he loved her and the kids, how much he appreciated her and stuff, how sorry he was that the Footlocker thing worked out the way it did, sorry that he let everybody down. The truth of the matter is that he and Heather had known it was coming. The district manager had warned him to shape up. He had offered to let Shun step down to assistant manager. But Shun was determined to make it. He wasn't going to take a pay cut, no way. He went to Home Depot and spent his own money on shelving for the stockroom. Heather helped with the backlog of paperwork. In the end, of course, it was useless. When Shun first called Heather to tell her the horrible news, the words he chose were these: *It finally happened.*

To find the mixer, Shun turned to his computer, an old Dell wedged between the wall and his side of the bed. Over the next few days, Shun spent a considerable amount of time searching online, most of it during the children's afternoon naps, the only free time in his day, time he might have better used studying for one of the four finals he has coming up this week—sociology, psychology, criminal justice, and history—or writing one of the two term papers that are due, one of which he's actually finding pretty interesting, about the history of segregation in his home state.

At last he found it. A black one just like she wanted. "Refurbished, like new, with only a couple of small scratches." Cost: $174. "They had some older ones that were less money, but I knew she'd love it," Shun says. "I was like, *Wrap that bad boy up.*"

And then Addison woke up screaming, which in turn woke Jackson. In his haste, Shun forgot to click the option for gift wrapping.

***

Another day, same scene: the condo, the couch, the clock on the wall with Roman numerals, battery-powered, *tick tick tick*, the gurgling of the eighteen-gallon aquarium, the water algae-green, the fish sluggish (two danios and a large tiger barb named Jake). Looking down from above the couch is a poster-sized watercolor portrait of a woman holding a rose, titled *Imperfection*. Shun painted it during his tenure as president of the Art Honor Society at West Jones High.

Shun and the kids have just returned from a brief outing. Jackson is on the floor, playing with his toy cars. When he's feeling well, as he is this afternoon, he is bright, engaging, cuddly, amusing. No hint of the demon seed of the days and nights before. Shun worries sometimes that Jackson has a split personality, that he's manic, hyper... *something*. He doesn't like to eat. He wakes up at night shrieking for his mom. Whenever he doesn't want to do something, he complains that part of him hurts—his foot, his tummy, his head. It's as if he enjoys being sick, weirdly craves it. Shun listens to the mothers on the playground, albeit from a distance. Every kid seems to have something these days, a *diagnosis*. Heather tells him his fears are unnecessary; she got her bachelor's in childhood development. She has further advised Shun that Jackson is perfectly fine, a normal little boy who gets clingy and moody when he's sick, who doesn't listen, who loses control. *Hello? He's only three! Of course he doesn't make any sense.* Heather would like Shun to go a little easy on the Sergeant Daddy routine. Choose your battles, she suggests. Does Jackson really have to eat that one last bite of hamburger before he's allowed to watch *The Doodlebops* on television?

And then there is Addison: good-natured, low maintenance, her chin slick with drool, *suck suck suck*. At the moment, she is suspended upright in the sling of one of those round plastic activity-center thingies, an ExerSaucer by Evenflo. Each of the brightly colored protuberances that Addison can push, turn, slide, or toggle makes a different musical noise. She pushes and pokes the buttons, delighted. Again and again and again.

Shun is sprawled on the couch, watching *The Tyra Banks Show*. Three finals down, sociology paper completed (a comparison of the number of doctors' offices versus liquor stores in rich versus poor areas of town). His history paper, due tonight, is awaiting a final proofing by Heather. Also up tonight: a five-minute in-class presentation on his paper topic, followed by a final essay. The professor is an older black man who lived through the days of segregation in central Florida. Shun likes and respects him. Though he enrolled in college to get a diploma, he is beginning to understand what is mean by *getting an education*; he can feel his horizons widening. The professor was vague about tonight's essay prompt. All he would say was that they couldn't study. That is fine with Shun, because he doesn't have any time to study. And no inclination, either. He is pooped. Whipped. Beat. *Assed out*, as they say in the Marines. After tonight, no classes again for six weeks. *Ooo-rah*.

Since Heather is supposed to take cookies to Jackson's school tomorrow, Shun has planned to give her the mixer tonight, when she comes home from work. He has removed it from its hiding place in the carport. Gift wrapped, complete with red ribbon, it sits next to him on the sofa as he watches Tyra Banks.

The camera zooms close, framing Tyra's sparkling eyes and milk-chocolate décolletage. Tyra looks good. *Goo-ood*. Maybe it's just boredom, whatever, lack of anything better to focus on, but, Heather complains, Shun is always horny. "He would like it every single day," Heather says. "Three or four times a day would be okay with him. Every time he touches me, or looks at me, or just brushes past, it's always like, 'I wanna have sex.' But I'm like, 'Could you please just get that out of your mind for a minute? Because I'm tired and I have a headache,' or whatever it is at that minute. Just leave me alone. And then when we finally *do* do it, it takes me much longer than him. And then he's always like, 'Well, if you give it to me more often...' and I just laugh. Sometimes, you know, I tell him, 'Go downstairs and take care of yourself.'"

Just then, the sound of a key in the door. The knob turns. Shun checks the clock: 3:35 p.m.

"Mommy!" trills Jackson.

"Mmmmmmmmmm!" gurgles Addison.

Heather steps into the condo, hangs her keys on the hook, puts her purse down on the table. Hands on hips, she takes stock: Shun sprawled, Tyra on TV, a load of dirty laundry sitting on the overstuffed chair that they both hate, the cat sleeping on top. She gives him a look.

"Surprise inspection, huh?" There is a guilty sound to his voice, even though he has nothing to feel guilty about, unless fantasizing is a crime, in which case all married men are guilty.

Heather kneels to hug Jackson, who is wrapped around her knees. She is wearing the new pants she bought the other night at Old Navy, marked down to $6.97.

This morning, as she was driving to work—the commute, she is finding, isn't so bad if you leave yourself enough time—Heather was doing a lot of thinking. After a month at the two hospitals, she is still a part-time substitute. The good news is that she's jumped right back into her field as if she'd never left; her superiors agree that she is doing an excellent job—always ten minutes early, *i*'s dotted and *t*'s crossed, comfortable with the patients in a hostile setting, familiar with available resources. She is working just under forty hours a week now, making roughly what Shun was making before he was fired. It still isn't really enough, but at least it's steady. The bad news is that she's already been turned down for a full-time job because she doesn't speak Spanish. People are telling her to stay positive: Something will come up.

Driving through the traffic, sipping from her Starbucks mug, Heather contemplated going back to school to study *español*. She used to speak it with her friends' parents; how long could it take to relearn? But then she thought, *You know what? If I'm gonna be the one providing for the family, maybe I want to be making a little more money than I am now. Maybe I want to be in a different position than I am now. I've always wanted to go to medical school. That's really, like, my dream. Why should I be standing around taking orders from doctors all day when I'd rather be one? Originally, I thought I'd wait until the kids were older, but maybe I could make it work now instead of waiting. I'm only twenty-eight. After eight years of training, I'll still be young enough to practice for a pretty long time....*

Before Shun was fired, everything had been perfect. That's really how Heather felt. Upon completing that first internship, the one that started two weeks after her C-section, and then another one the next semester, she was awarded her master's degree. And then she made a big decision. She would stay home and raise Jackson, who would be her only child.

As the months went by, however, Heather's heart began to change. She'd always wanted a girl. Having one kid was *so* great. How much harder could it be with two? As she always did with one of their home-improvement projects, the first thing Heather did was go out and buy a book, *How to Have a Girl*, by J.M. Young. Per usual, Heather worked diligently toward her goal, keeping charts of her temperature, checking regularly the viscosity of her mucus, eating healthy foods, the works. Shun helped, too.

And they know exactly when it happened: Heather called Shun to tell him to come home from work immediately. It was the only other time in his life that Jackson has been left with a babysitter.

The next thing she knew, Heather was waking up each blue California morning with two kids in the condo, and it was good. She'd make plans for their day, go to the park, to museums, do the errands and the laundry, clean the house, no problem. She loved it. She loved her kids; she was part of their lives every minute of every day. And best of all, she was the absolute queen of her domain. She set the rules, the schedules, the agenda. Everything was totally under her control. It was awesome.

But then again, she had also gotten to the point where she was kind of wanting a little more time of her own. Time away. Time to be herself, to further her goals, of which there have always been many. She hated being this helpless woman who needed a man to support her. Because Shun was on commission—as manager, along with his salary, he drew a percentage of sales—his check varied from month to month. She never felt really secure. As the family bill payer, she was always juggling. "Our credit cards were our best friends," she says ruefully.

Even when Shun was in his heyday with Footlocker, Heather never really felt as if they had a cushion. She is not one to complain; she doesn't have a lot, she doesn't need a lot, she's never been one of those women. But truthfully, she never felt as if she could buy herself anything, either. Granted, with Jackson, she bought every little baby and toddler thing you could possibly buy. That didn't last long. Fifty grand just didn't go very far. Luckily, they'd bought the condo at the right time, in 2000, for $132,500. (Though when they bought it, it felt like a huge rip-off.) It has more than doubled in value in six years. But that is money on paper, not money you can spend. They lived okay, didn't deprive the kids of anything. But they never spent anything on themselves. She bought nothing, really, no makeup, no new clothes, maybe just a pair of sweatpants from the Gap on clearance. Shun cut his own hair. She had her hair cut only every six or eight months, never had it highlighted like her friends. And pedicures: Oh. My. God. *Pedicures.* How she loves them—the foot massage, the vibrating chair, the lush feeling of total self-indulgence. If she had money, she would get one every week. *Every week. That* would be success to Heather. That's how it would feel to her, a thirty-dollar pedicure every week. That and a new place to live, of course, their own house, not too large, say 1,800 square feet—a place where more than one person could go potty at one time. And a little bit of travel maybe, as long as she's on the subject. She grew up thirty-five minutes north of San Francisco. The first time she saw the city, she was sixteen. Total list of places she's been in her life: Oregon, Mississippi, Texas, Arizona. She'd love to go to the East Coast. To New York. To Maine. To New Hampshire. She'd love to see the leaves change.

Maybe when I'm a doctor I'll make enough money so we can do some of that stuff, she thought to herself, commuting to work, applying lip gloss as she inched along the exit ramp. And then she thought, *One thing's for sure: I'm never gonna not have an income again. Not after what happened this time. I'm too anal for that. I need more control.* And then she started thinking about medical school, about where she might go, how she might pay for it, how it would play out... and that's when it hit her: her student loans! College and grad school: $45,000. She's supposed to start paying them off this year. Oh. My. God. *Note to self: apply for extension of forbearance, due to economic hardship.* At 2 percent interest, why hurry?

Now, in the condo, home early from work, meaning fewer hours this week, less money, Heather spies the gift-wrapped box on the sofa. "What's that?"

Shun raises an eyebrow. "Something for you."

She takes a seat in the glider rocker. He sets the heavy, cube-shaped package on top of the ottoman. She looks at him archly: It's not a KitchenAid, is it?"

Totally busted: "You're smarter than the average bear."

"You keep asking me to make you cookies," a slightly condescending tone, *you big galoot*. She pulls off the wrapping paper, confirms her suspicion. Her lips tighten with disapproval.

"But not just any KitchenAid," Shun sings brightly, *ta da*, playing the pitchman, trying to keep the applecart upright. "It's... a *refurbished* KitchenAid."

"Refurbished?"

"Like new."

"From Overstock.com?"

"Amazon."

She turns the box over, reading each side. Some of the writing is in *español*.

"Why are you trying to read the box?" Shun asks, annoyed. "I just told you where it came from."

"I wanna know what *color* it is," she snaps back.

"It's green. What do you think? It's harvest gold."

She opens the top. "It's black," she says, obviously tickled.

"To match the coffeemaker." He aims his face toward hers, seeking eye contact: "Just like you always wanted, right?"

Now Jackson comes over to inspect the box. Heather removes the mixer. It is a huge thing, sleek and black, as if made from the same material as a stealth bomber. Heather pats her son on the butt with a cupped palm, lets it linger there. "With this machine, Jackson, you could make cookies all by yourself."

Jackson's face crumbles. "I don't *wanna* make cookies by myself!"

She pulls the five-quart bowl out of the box, places it on the cradle. An upbeat, mommy voice: "All you do is put everything in there and then press the button. It's simple."

"*I don't wanna make cookies by myself!*"

At last she meets her husband's eyes. "Thanks, Shun."

"Sure, babycakes." He gives her one of his big, big smiles.

But then he notices. Something's not right. She doesn't look happy or thankful. Not one bit. "What's wrong?" he asks.

"I thought we weren't gonna get each other any presents."

"It was cheap."

"How cheap?"

He straightens himself, voice deep and confident. "The *original* price was $300. I got it for $174."

She eyeballs him. "That's not cheap."

"How much you wanna bet?"

"One hundred and seventy-four dollars." She pronounces each word clearly. "On a *mixer*."

"Yeah..." he says, his tone uncertain. "On a mixer for *you*."

"My hand can do $174 worth of mixing."

"No, you can't."

"Yeah. I *can*."

"Mommy?"

"Yes, Jackson?"

"Can we make cookies now, Mommy?"

"Not right now, Jackson." She puts the KitchenAid back in the box. "Mommy's gonna go take a shower."

***

Bedtime now, one month later, 9:00 on a Sunday night. There are two bedrooms upstairs in the condo and one full bath, small enough that you can spit in the sink while sitting on the toilet. All of the Ducksworths are wearing their jammies.

Jackson is in the master bedroom, eleven by thirteen feet, playing on the computer. Everyone else is in the smaller room that the kids share, Jackson's big-guy bed along one wall, Addison's crib along the other. For the past three weeks, while Shun's parents were visiting from Soso, Heather and Shun were sleeping here in the kids' room, on a queen-size AeroBed. On the penultimate night of their exile, the AeroBed sprang a leak. They all four awoke on the floor.

Addison is playing with toys, which means putting first one thing in her mouth and then another. In a couple of minutes, she will pull herself up by the crib's leg and start making her way via handholds around the room—a sign she is almost ready to walk. Next household project: childproofing. It will be the last time. Shun had the snip a few months ago.

As part of their childproofing efforts, Heather has ordered something for Addison's crib called a bumper. It serves the same purpose as the padding around a goalpost. One side effect of the cruising stage is a lot of falling down. Addison has two big welts on her forehead; Heather keeps making nervous jokes about somebody calling Child Protective Services, which is what she sometimes has to do in her capacity at the hospital. Included with the bumper, which was ordered online, is a matching dust ruffle, another of the many and varied household necessities that Shun doesn't understand the need for—as if that mattered. To install the ruffle, the crib had to be virtually disassembled. That job was his.

Now Heather is bent over the reassembled crib, tying the little ribbons from the bumper around the slats. Shun is on his knees, folding laundry, putting it away in drawers. As she works, Heather is talking about the future, a subject she very much enjoys. Heather is a planner. She wants to know who, what, where, and what time—as far in advance as possible. She wants to put it on her calendar, in ink, so she can be certain of what to expect next; in this way, she can be sure to arrive her usual ten minutes early. Shun is just the opposite. Invariably, when they're driving somewhere in their Odyssey minivan, on a longish trip, there will come a moment when the kids will finally be asleep and Heather will ask, "Where do you see yourself in five years?" Shun always has the same answer: "Don't bother me while I'm drivin'."

So, tying the bumper to the crib, Heather is talking about *her* vision of the future, this one involving possible renovations to their condo. A washer and dryer would make life easier; it's disgusting to wash your clothes in a machine where strangers' underwear has been. Another idea is to finish the attic; some people in their complex have built lofts up there, adding to their square footage by nearly 50 percent. The only problem: You'd need a ladder to get to it.

"I'm thinking that might not work," opines Shun, folding one of Addison's little shirts with his big hands, laying it carefully in the drawer.

Heather shrugs dismissively. "In two years, I wanna move out of here anway. Three tops."

Shun looks up at her from his place on the floor. There is a hurt expression on his brown, papa-bear face.

"What?" Heather asks, clueless.

"There you go again," he says.

"What do you mean?"

Shun looks at her, not sure how far to push. For the most part, these last few weeks have been pretty okay. School was out; his parents were here to help take care of the kids. It was good to see them, especially his dad, who'd had a heart bypass two months before Shun got fired. When Norman got sick, it hit Shun hard. For the first time, it dawned on him: He was less than eight years from forty. *Man, the time really goes quick.*

Meanwhile, Heather's job prospects continue to look good. She has been subbing mostly at one hospital now, getting five full days a week. Combined with the money she makes doing the books at the chiropractor's office—the people keep begging her to stay—they are doing all right financially. And more good news: After eight months without health insurance, Heather and Shun have finally been accepted by Blue Cross, $350 a month, with no restrictions on treatment for Heather's allergies and asthma. Overall, with their restructured debt, they probably have a few more dollars in their pockets now than they had when Shun was working.

The only real negative thing that has surfaced is Shun's grades: one B, one C, two D's. The D in psychology was his second in the same course; he'd taken it previously, hoping to get a jump start on his freshman workload. The other D was in criminal justice, which is what he was thinking of majoring in, though he doesn't need to declare a major until the beginning of his junior year. The problem is, you don't get credit for D's. He'll have to take both courses again. All that time and money, completely wasted.

When Heather first went online to check Shun's grades—he hadn't shown any inclination to check them himself—she was very surprised, to say the least. There had to be a mistake. She was like, "You went every day, you attended classes, you participated in class discussions—isn't any of that taken into account?" Maybe there was some wiggle room, she thought, a point or two somewhere to be found, enough to get him up to a C, so he could get the credits and move on. Email your teachers, she urged him. Tell them about your situation. It's called grade grubbing, she explained—a very important part of college academics. "The worst they can do is say no," she said.

"I asked him, 'Do you wanna go back to work? Do you want to find a job?'" Heather says. "But he's like, 'No, I don't.' And I said, 'Well then, you better figure out how you're gonna continue in school, because you can't take a semester off, because then it'll take you even longer. And you can't really go to work, because I'm working, and we don't want the kids in daycare.' I told him, 'We all have something to hold up in order to make everything work. I'm holding up my end of the deal here. You're not holding up yours.'"

Shun's reply: "I know Heather has a point, but I think that's my problem and stuff. I know it's just a simple email she wants me to write and stuff, but I still haven't done it. I don't know why. It's not that I'm putting it off. I'm not even... Well, it's just not a priority for me. Maybe I should, you know, but I just don't. I don't feel like I should piss and moan about my grades. I feel like I should have done better, and that's it.

"I'm still committed to the college route. It's not like Heather's forcing me. It's something I've always wanted to do. If you ask me about my biggest regret in life, it's that I didn't go to college. It was just that after high school, nobody was encouraging me to go. Nobody said, 'You should really go to college.' Then I had the whole break from school, the Marines. Trying to get back into college mode was hard for me. There's a little pressure. It's tough with the kids.

"By getting a degree, I'll be able to support my family better. That is my first priority. I still want to go the criminal-justice route, but I don't want to do anything that'll be too hazardous. Like, part of me wants to be a cop, I could see myself—I mean, I wouldn't mind falling back into that whole military-type role. I would probably still be in the Marines if it wasn't for Heather; she didn't want to live that life, and I can't blame her. I could go into forensics. That's pretty cool: CSI, you know. Or corrections: I could work in a prison—though you have to literally stay in the prison for several days at a time. I can't see doing that, not right now, anyway. That's the thing—the kids. I used to work all the time, so I missed them and stuff, but I didn't really know them. Now I'm used to seeing them every minute. I'm attached. I don't like to miss out on stuff. So it's kind of like a big catch-22."

Now, back in the kids' room, Heather is staring down at her husband, upon whose dark and handsome face is probably the most deflated, defeated, wrenchingly vulnerable expression she has ever seen grace his countenance. She feels her throat catch: "What?" she beseeches. "What is it?"

He looks at her reproachfully. "You said *I*."

"What do you mean?"

"You said: 'In two years, I wanna move out of here.'"

"And?"

"And..."

"Do *you* want to be living here in two years?"

"You said *I* instead of *we*."

Dumbstruck, Heather stares at her husband of almost six years. Stacey LaShun Ducksworth: the guy who refused to do it with her because she'd had too much to drink. Her only lover since she was eighteen—though she did kiss a guy once in Tijuana, another Marine, a black guy, no less, when she and Shun were temporarily broken up. It was the only other time she had known Shun to cry. *Such a good man*, she thinks. *A great husband, a great dad.* He does so many things right. He just doesn't have the—she doesn't know what to call it, the thing he's lacking. The drive to compete, maybe, the drive to be better than others, to run in front of the pack instead of in the middle. For him, it's always like, *Status quo: Great, this is working for us.* For her, it's always like, *No, it's not. How do we make it better?* Says

Heather: "His purpose in this world isn't just to be a husband and a dad. You can't do everything for everyone else. You can't be okay with that. Every person needs something of their own, a goal to accomplish that doesn't have anything to do with anyone else. You have to do stuff for yourself. That's my thing: What's your goal?"

Heather smiles at him. "I'm sorry. I didn't mean to say *I*."

"Well, you did. You do it all the time."

They look at each other for a moment, considering, and then Heather laughs. "I do *not* do it *all* the time," she says dismissively, like maybe she knows she does but is not about to let on. She bends back down over the crib, proceeds to tie the remaining bumper ribbons.

Shun returns to folding clothes, putting them in the drawer, grumbling silently to himself—*Yeah, right*—as husbands do, knowing full well you can't get into trouble for things you don't say aloud.

***

"Who asked who first?" Shun challenges. The kids are asleep. There is a large, goofy, cat-ate-the-canary smile on his face.

"You did," Heather says, somewhat dubiously.

He looks at her with hooded eyes. "Okay, so now I'm lyin'?"

"No... it's just like... you make it seem like I came to you with a ring and stuff."

"Who asked who first?" Shun repeats.

"You said, 'If you ask me to marry you, then I'll ask you.'"

"Who asked who first?"

"So I said, 'Fine, will you marry me?'"

"Who asked who first then?"

"I asked you."

"Exactly. You asked me to marry you."

"But I didn't ask you in a *formal manner*," Heather clarifies.

"It don't matter, formal or informal. *Who asked who first?*"

"Jeez, Louise!"

"Don't bring *her* into this now."

"*Fiiiine.*"

Long pause.
Then Shun speaks: "So tell me: Who asked who?"
"I didn't deny it."
"Exactly."

Permissions

The following stories were first published in a different form in *Esquire*: "The Marine," December, 2001. "Wounded Warriors" (as "Wounded Battalion"), December, 2007. "Vetville," July 2011. "Fifty Grand in San Diego," July 2016.

» "The Marine," was published in *Revenge of the Donut Boys* (Da Capo Press, The Sager Group LLC) © 2008, 2018 by Mike Sager

» "Wounded Warriors," was previously. published in *Wounded Warriors* (Da Capo Press) © 2008 by Mike Sager

» "Vetville" was previously published in *The Someone You're Not* (The Sager Group LLC) © 2012 by Mike Sager

» "Fifty Grand in San Diego" was published in *Revenge of the Donut Boys* (Da Capo Press, The Sager Group LLC) © 2008, 2018 by Mike Sager

About the Author

Mike Sager is a bestselling author and award-winning reporter. For more than forty years he has worked primarily as a writer for the *Washington Post*, *Rolling Stone*, *GQ* and *Esquire*. Sager is the author or editor of more than a dozen books, including anthologies, novels, a biography, eBooks, and textbooks. In 2010 he won the National Magazine Award for profile writing. Several of his stories have inspired films and documentaries; he is editor and publisher of The Sager Group LLC. For more information, please see www.MikeSager.com.

More Books From This Author

- » *The Lonely Hedonist*
- » *Stoned Again*
- » *The Devil and John Holmes*
- » *High Tolerance, A Novel*
- » *The Someone You're Not*
- » *Revenge of the Donut Boys*
- » *Scary Monsters and Super Freaks*
- » *Hunting Marlon Brando*

About the Publisher

The Sager Group was founded in 1984. In 2012 it was chartered as a multimedia content brand, with the intent of empowering those who create art — an umbrella beneath which makers can pursue, and profit from, their craft directly, without gatekeepers. TSG publishes books; ministers to artists and provides modest grants; designs logos, products and packaging, and produces documentary, feature, and commercial films. By harnessing the means of production, The Sager Group helps artists help themselves. To read more from The Sager Group, please see www.MikeSager.com.

Artifex Te Adiuva

Made in the USA
San Bernardino, CA
12 July 2020

75382827R00105